S0-BSX-461

THE MARVELS PROJECT

BIRTH OF THE SUPER HEROES

THE MARVELS PROJECT: BIRTH OF THE SUPER HEROES. Contains material originally published in magazine form as THE MARVELS PROJECT #1-8. First printing 2010. ISBN# 978-0-7851-4630-8. Published by MARVEL WORLDWIDE, INC., a subsidiary of MARVEL ENTERTAINMENT, LLC. OFFICE OF PUBLICATION: 417 5th Avenue, New York, NY 10016. Copyright © 2009 and 2010 Marvel Characters, Inc. All rights reserved. $34.99 per copy in the U.S. and $39.99 in Canada (GST #R127032852); Canadian Agreement #40668537. All characters featured in this issue and the distinctive names and likenesses thereof, and all related indicia are trademarks of Marvel Characters, Inc. No similarity between any of the names, characters, persons, and/or institutions in this magazine with those of any living or dead person or institution is intended, and any such similarity which may exist is purely coincidental. **Printed in the U.S.A.** ALAN FINE, EVP - Office of the President, Marvel Worldwide, Inc. and EVP & CMO Marvel Characters B.V.; DAN BUCKLEY, Chief Executive Officer and Publisher - Print, Animation & Digital Media; JIM SOKOLOWSKI, Chief Operating Officer; DAVID GABRIEL, SVP of Publishing Sales & Circulation; DAVID BOGART, SVP of Business Affairs & Talent Management; MICHAEL PASCIULLO, VP Merchandising & Communications; JIM O'KEEFE, VP of Operations & Logistics; DAN CARR, Executive Director of Publishing Technology; JUSTIN F. GABRIE, Director of Publishing & Editorial Operations; SUSAN CRESPI, Editorial Operations Manager; ALEX MORALES, Publishing Operations Manager; STAN LEE, Chairman Emeritus. For information regarding advertising in Marvel Comics or on Marvel.com, please contact Ron Stern, VP of Business Development, at rstern@marvel.com. For Marvel subscription inquiries, please call 800-217-9158. **Manufactured between 6/14/10 and 7/14/10** by WORLDCOLOR PRESS INC., VERSAILLES, KY, USA.

10 9 8 7 6 5 4 3 2 1

THE MARVELS PROJECT

BIRTH OF THE SUPER HEROES

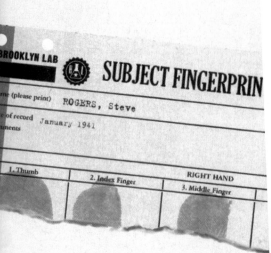

BROOKLYN LAB

PROJECTS DIVISION

Writer: Ed Brubaker
Artist: Steve Epting
Color Art: Dave Stewart • Letters: VC's Chris Eliopoulos
Covers: Steve Epting; Gerald Parel; Steve McNiven with Dexter
Vines, Dean White & Justin Ponsor; Phil Jimenez with Morry
Hollowell; and Alan Davis with Mark Farmer & Javier Rodriguez
Variant Trade Dress designed by Rian Hughes
Associate Editors: Jeanine Schaefer & Lauren Sankovitch
Editor: Tom Brevoort

* * *

1939 DAILY BUGLE:
Head Writer: John Rhett Thomas
Writers: Jess Harrold, Sheila Johnson, Dugan Trodglen & Jeph York
Artist: Chance Fiveash • Cover Artist: Mike Mayhew
Layout: Brian O'Dell • Research: Bob Greenberger

* * *

Collection Editor: Mark D. Beazley
Editorial Assistants: James Emmett & Joe Hochstein
Assistant Editor: Alex Starbuck
Associate Editor: John Denning
Editor, Special Projects: Jennifer Grünwald
Senior Editor, Special Projects: Jeff Youngquist
Research: Jeph York
Book Designer: Michael Chatham
Senior Vice President of Sales: David Gabriel

* * *

Editor in Chief: Joe Quesada
Publisher: Dan Buckley
Executive Producer: Alan Fine

The Marvels Project # 1 Cover by Steve Epting

PROLOGUE
NEW YORK--1938.

SEE, WHEN I GOT OLD...THEY SENT ME *BACK*...

BACK TO MY HOME...IN MY *OWN* TIME...

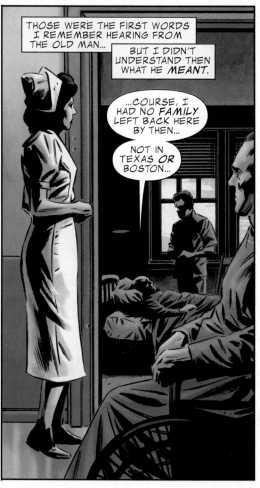

THOSE WERE THE FIRST WORDS I REMEMBER HEARING FROM THE OLD MAN...

BUT I DIDN'T UNDERSTAND THEN WHAT HE *MEANT*.

...COURSE, I HAD NO *FAMILY* LEFT BACK HERE BY THEN...

NOT IN TEXAS *OR* BOSTON...

AND ANYWAY...NEW YORK...IT ALL BEGINS HERE ANYWAY...

...I HOPE TO BE AROUND... FOR THAT...

CA-HAAKK! HACCKK!

EASY, MISTER HAWK...IT'S OKAY.

I *SHOULD* HAVE, TOO. I SHOULD HAVE KNOWN IMMEDIATELY WHO *MATT HAWK* WAS.

BUT INSTEAD, HE WAS JUST ANOTHER OLD MAN I WAS HOPING TO LEARN FROM.

YOU DON'T *KNOW*...NONE OF YOU DO, WHAT'S COMING...

THE *THINGS* I'VE SEEN...OUT THERE...

HE'D TELL ME OF THE *FUTURE* ON THOSE LONG AFTERNOONS, OF LIFE BEYOND THE DEPRESSION...

BECAUSE HE'D *BEEN THERE*, HE WOULD INSIST.

HE'D TALK OF GODS AND MONSTERS AND HEROES WITH SHIELDS AND ARMOR.

I WOULD JOT IT ALL DOWN IN MY NOTEBOOK AND NOD, TAKING IT ALL IN...

THESE PULP-TINGED FANTASIES WERE UNLIKE ANY CASE OF SENILE DEMENTIA I'D EVER HEARD...

...AND I GENUINELY LOOKED FORWARD TO MY VISITS WITH HIM.

OH, DR. HALLOWAY, YOU'RE HERE... *GOOD.*

YOU CAN SIGN THE *DEATH CERTIFICATE.*

HE WENT IN HIS *SLEEP...* SWEET OLD GUY...

YES...IT'S A *REAL* SHAME. HE WAS QUITE A CHARACTER.

OH, AND LAST NIGHT HE ASKED ME TO GIVE YOU *THIS...*

LAST NIGHT?

IT'S STRANGE... BUT...

...HE SEEMED TO *KNOW* HE WOULDN'T BE WAKING UP.

WHEN I OPENED THE BOX, I UNDERSTOOD IMMEDIATELY.

I DIDN'T EVEN HAVE TO READ THE CARD HE'D LEFT.

NO... TOM... YOU FOOL.

For Dr. Thomas Halloway

MATTHEW HAWK. FROM BOSTON AND TEXAS. A LAWYER.

MATT HAWK WAS THE TWO-GUN KID.

I'D READ EVERYTHING ABOUT THE TWO-GUN KID GROWING UP.

TOMBSTONE'S MASKED GUN-FIGHTER. A TRUE WESTERN HERO.

BUT, OF COURSE, I'D READ *EVERYTHING* IN THE ENTIRE *PRISON LIBRARY* GROWING UP.

AND EVERY OTHER BOOK MY FATHER, *THE WARDEN*, BROUGHT TO MY CONCRETE ROOM IN THAT EMPTY CELL BLOCK.

STILL, I CURSED MYSELF AGAIN.

I COULD HAVE TOLD THIS DYING HERO WHAT HIS EXPLOITS, HOWEVER FICTIONAL, HAD MEANT TO ME...

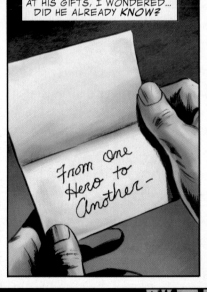

BUT WHEN I LOOKED AT HIS GIFTS, I WONDERED... DID HE ALREADY *KNOW?*

From One to Hero to Another—

AND SUDDENLY, THE FUTURE... THE WORLD THAT OLD MISTER HAWK HAD TOLD ME ABOUT...

IT DIDN'T SEEM SO FAR AWAY.

PART ONE
THE ATLANTIC OCEAN—1939.

BEFORE AMERICA WAS AT WAR, FDR OFTEN TOOK PRESIDENTIAL VACATIONS ON THE YACHT OF MILLIONAIRE VINCENT ASTOR.

AN OLD FRIEND OF THE PRESIDENT, ASTOR ALSO RAN A SECRET INTELLIGENCE GROUP KNOWN AS *THE ROOM*.

I SAY IT'S *SOLID*, FRANK. IT'S WORTH RISKING SOLDIERS TO FIND OUT FOR SURE. WE'VE GOT A *CHANCE* OF STOPPING THIS *PROJECT NIETZSCHE* OF THEIRS...

OKAY, KERMIT...GET *SAWYER* WORKING ON A PLAN.

I'M AFRAID THERE'S BAD NEWS ON OUR *OWN* SCIENTIFIC FRONT, MISTER PRESIDENT.

THE *BROOKLYN* LAB? WE'RE FINANCING THAT THROUGH YOUR *BACK-CHANNELS*, RIGHT, VINCE?

THE CREATURE KEEPS CATCHING *FIRE*.

YES, IT'S ALL UNDER THE RUG, MR. PRESIDENT...BUT IT MAY ALL BE A WASTE, TOO.

IT KEEPS *WHAT?*

THEY'RE *WORKING* ON IT, PROFESSOR HORTON AND HIS PARTNER... WHAT'S HIS NAME-- *BRADLEY.*

IT'S AN *AMAZING* BREAKTHROUGH, EVEN AT THIS STAGE.

...IT KEEPS *CATCHING FIRE...*

A SYNTHETIC MAN WHO LIGHTS ON FIRE *COULD* BE USEFUL IN *OTHER* WAYS.

MIGHT STARTLE THE GERMANS INTO MAKING A *MISTAKE...* GIVE US SOMETHING NEW TO GO ON.

THAT'S AN *INTERESTING* THOUGHT...

THE NAVY'S REPORTING SOME GERMAN SHIPS OUT IN THE ATLANTIC, HEADING TOWARD BERMUDA.

I *HEARD* THAT, TOO...WE DON'T KNOW WHAT THEY'RE UP TO...

...BUT THEY'RE DROPPING *DEPTH CHARGES* OUT THERE.

KA-SHOOOM

‹THIS MISSION... IT'S *WORSE* THAN I THOUGHT IT WOULD BE, HANS.›

‹JUST DO AS YOU'RE *TOLD*, TANNER...›

‹...YOU'LL SOON LEARN TO SEE THIS AS NOTHING MORE THAN *FISHING*.›

‹IF IT HELPS SOOTHE YOUR STOMACH, I OVERHEARD THE SCIENCE OFFICER YESTERDAY... THIS IS AN IMPORTANT JOB WE'RE DOING...›

‹THE STUDY OF THESE *CREATURES* IS IMPORTANT TO WORK BACK IN THE *FATHERLAND*...›

MIRELLA, STACIAN, AND RODIS WERE THEIR NAMES, HE WOULD TELL ME...LONG AFTER THEIR MURDER.

BUT IT WOULD BE MANY YEARS BEFORE *PRINCE NAMOR* WOULD ALLOW HIMSELF TO SPEAK OF THOSE DAYS.

NEIN! NEIN!

MEIN GOTT! NEIN!

THE DAYS WHEN HIS MOTHER'S *PROPHECIES* OF THE SURFACE-MEN'S *RETURN* WERE FINALLY COMING TO PASS.

WHEN THE *CURIOSITY* HE'D ALWAYS VIEWED HIS FATHER'S PEOPLE WITH...

...WAS REPLACED WITH THE *FURY* OF THE PRINCE OF A REALM *UNDER ATTACK.*

THE LORD OF A DWINDLING PEOPLE.

SO MANY...

SO MANY OF MINE...

YOU WILL PAY.

ALL OF YOU.

A FEW WEEKS AFTER THE PRESIDENT'S INTELLIGENCE BRIEFING, PROFESSOR PHINEAS HORTON UNVEILED HIS *SYNTHETIC MAN* IN BROOKLYN.

IT WAS A SHOW WORTHY OF P.T. BARNUM.

THE *ARTIFICIAL MAN* CAUGHT FIRE WHEN EXPOSED TO OXYGEN, AND THE PRESS WENT WILD.

FEW ARTICLES MENTIONED THAT HORTON'S PARTNER, DR. JAMES BRADLEY, HAD LEFT THE PROJECT BEFORE THE UNVEILING...

--WON'T HAVE MY WORK *WASTED* ON A *PUBLICITY STUNT!*

IT'S NOT A STUNT, IT WILL BE A REVELATION, BRADLEY. IT WILL *CHANGE THE WORLD.*

YOU'RE LETTING THEM *USE YOU*-- ROOSEVELT'S PEOPLE.

I'M DOING *NOTHING* OF THE KIND...

BUT...DID YOU NOT *REALIZE* WHO WE WERE *WORKING FOR* ALL THIS TIME?

THE GOVERNMENT HAD PLAYED THEIR HAND WELL, OR SO THEY THOUGHT.

PROFESSOR HORTON! WHAT IS THE CREATURE'S NAME?!

PROFESSOR! OVER HERE!

THE NEWS OF A "HUMAN TORCH" CREATED IN AN AMERICAN LAB WOULD SURELY GENERATE NEWS OVERSEAS...

...AND IN TURN PROVOKE A REACTION FROM THE GERMANS.

DESTROY THE FIRE-MAN! HE IS A CRIME AGAINST NATURE!

GOD MAKES MAN! DON'T MAKE MONSTERS!

DESTROY THE FIRE-MAN!

GOD MAKES MAN! DON'T...

NO MORE FIRE MAN!!

FIRE MAN IS A CRIME AGAINST NAT...

ONLY GOD. NOT MAN.

NO MORE FIRE MAN

SAVE US FROM

FIRE

BUT WHAT WASN'T COUNTED ON WAS THE REACTION IN THE CITY.

ENCASE HIM IN CEMENT?

I'M AFRAID THE PRESIDENT INSISTS...WE CAN'T HAVE PUBLIC UNREST LIKE THIS...

NOT AT SUCH A CRUCIAL TIME.

IT'S NOT REALLY A HIM, ANYWAY, IS IT?

IT'S MORE OF A WHAT.

CAN'T YOU SIMPLY TURN HIM OFF?

I'M SORRY, MY BOY...

THEY DON'T UNDERSTAND YOU.

OVER HORTON'S OBJECTIONS, THE CREATURE WAS BURIED IN TONS OF CONCRETE ON GOVERNMENT-OWNED PROPERTY IN NEW YORK CITY...

WHERE NEITHER OXYGEN NOR ENEMY SPIES COULD REACH HIM.

BUT, AS HOPED, WORD OF HIS EXISTENCE DID REACH GERMANY...

‹YOU'VE SEEN THIS ALREADY, I HOPE?›

DAILY BUGLE
FIRE-MAN IS ALIVE!

‹YES...AND THERE ARE NEWSREELS, TOO.›

DAI
Scientific Marvel Bursts Into Living Flame
FIRE-M
IS ALIV
SPARKLEBERRY

‹SO, WHAT DO YOU THINK, ERSKINE?›

‹I SUPPOSE THE S.S. ARE GOING TO BE EXERTING MORE PRESSURE ON US IF THIS IS REAL.›

‹I SUPPOSE.›

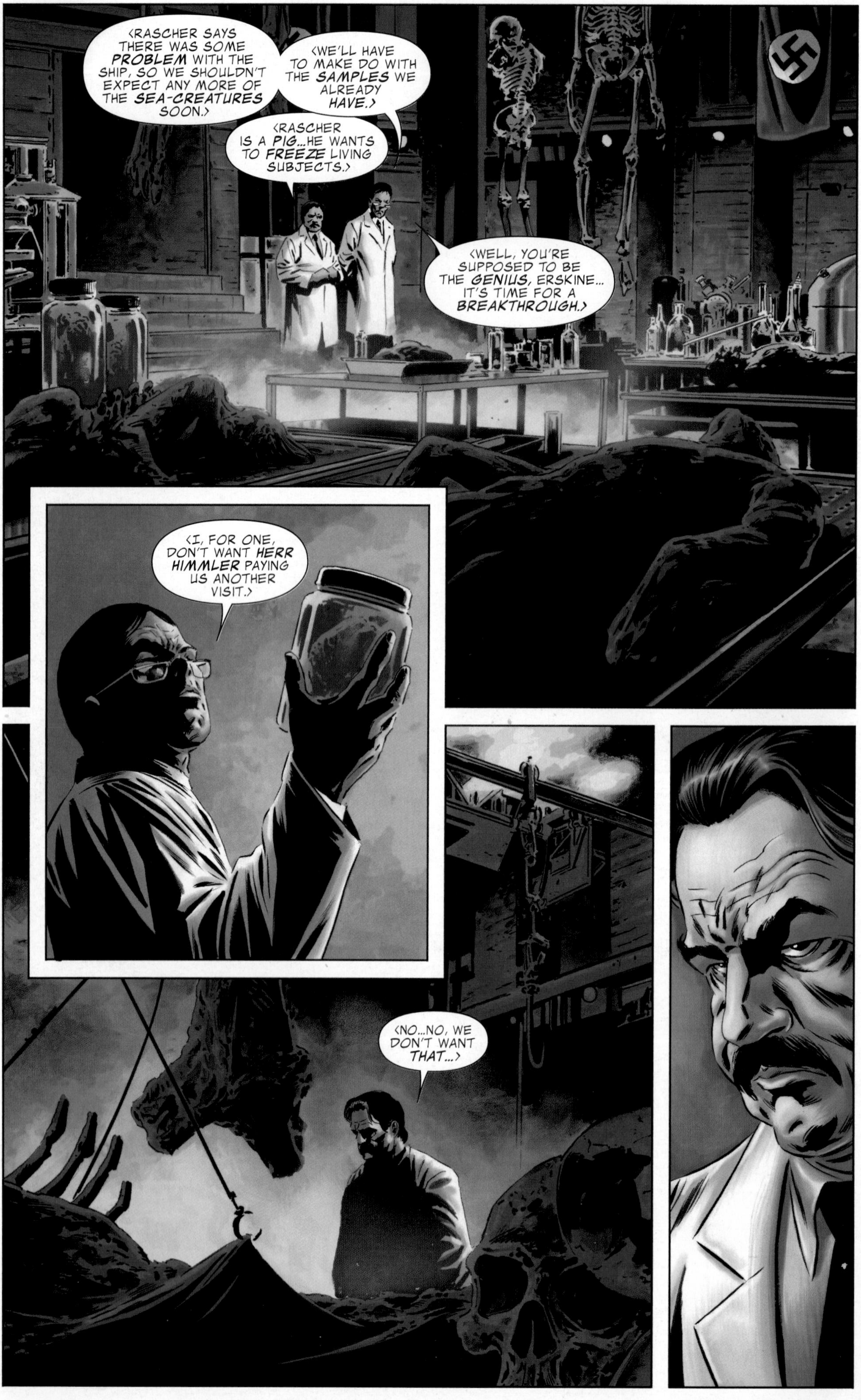
<RASCHER SAYS THERE WAS SOME PROBLEM WITH THE SHIP, SO WE SHOULDN'T EXPECT ANY MORE OF THE SEA-CREATURES SOON.>
<WE'LL HAVE TO MAKE DO WITH THE SAMPLES WE ALREADY HAVE.>
<RASCHER IS A PIG...HE WANTS TO FREEZE LIVING SUBJECTS.>
<WELL, YOU'RE SUPPOSED TO BE THE GENIUS, ERSKINE... IT'S TIME FOR A BREAKTHROUGH.>
<I, FOR ONE, DON'T WANT HERR HIMMLER PAYING US ANOTHER VISIT.>
<NO...NO, WE DON'T WANT THAT...>

LONDON, ENGLAND.

THE WIRES FILLED WITH *CHATTER* THAT WEEK... MOST UNABLE TO BE DECODED BY THE AGENTS WHO INTERCEPTED IT...

BUT EVERYONE *KNEW* WHAT THEY WERE TALKING ABOUT.

...X MEANS B, THEN...THIS MEANS...THIS...

AND THERE WAS ONE SIGNAL THAT CAME THROUGH LOUD AND CLEAR...

THIS...NO, IF THIS IS THE *REAL THING*...BY GOD...

WHAT *IS IT*, PERVIS?

I NEED TO GET BACK TO *HOME OFFICE*...

...THEY AND *OUR AMERICAN FRIEND* WILL WANT TO *SEE THIS* STRAIGHT AWAY.

BACK IN NEW YORK, THERE WAS A TENSION IN THE AIR YOU COULD ALMOST FEEL.

WE'D BEEN TOLD THE *FLAMING MAN* HAD BEEN *DESTROYED*...BUT THERE WERE RUMORS THE ENTIRE THING HAD BEEN A *HOAX*.

WHAT CLEARLY WASN'T A *HOAX*, THOUGH...WAS *HITLER'S* MARCH ACROSS EUROPE.

THE NAZI WAR MACHINE WAS A HORROR TO BEHOLD... AND EVEN THOUGH WE WERE AN OCEAN AWAY...

IT DIDN'T FEEL LIKE WE WERE SAFE.

IT DIDN'T FEEL LIKE THIS WAR WOULDN'T TOUCH US.

IT FELT LIKE WE WERE JUST BIDING OUR TIME.

AND IN A WAY, WE PROBABLY WERE...

THAT'S THEM? THOSE TWO?

IT IS.

THEY LOOK LIKE A COUPLE OF YAHOOS.

WELL, THEY ARE AMERICANS, LIEUTENANT.

OH, NO YOU DON'T, RED.

I SAW HER FIRST!

WE'RE NOT IN P.S. 109 ANYMORE, NICK...YOU CAN'T CALL DIBS ON A DAME.

I'M TELLIN' YOU...DON'T EVEN THINK ABOUT IT, MISTER.

I DON'T KNOW... LET'S KEEP LOOKING.

I ASSURE YOU, THEY'RE QUITE GOOD...

THEY'VE BEEN HELPING TRAIN OUR PARATROOPERS FOR MONTHS.

RIGHT! ENOUGH OF THIS NONSENSE.

OH... COLONEL ELLIS...

LISTEN UP, BOYS, I'VE BEEN ASKED TO MAKE AN INTRODUCTION...

...AND I'LL THANK YOU NOT TO MAKE ME LOOK LIKE A FOOL FOR DOING SO.

NICK FURY AND RED HARGROVE, MEET ANOTHER OF YOUR COUNTRYMEN...LIEUTENANT SAWYER.

HE'S HERE TO OFFER YOU A JOB.

ASSUMING YOU CAN STOP DRINKING AND FIGHTING LONG ENOUGH TO FOLLOW ORDERS.

BUT THE COLONEL HERE SAYS YOU CAN.

LOOK, NO OFFENSE, LIEUTENANT...BUT WHAT THE HELL IS *UNCLE SAM* DOIN' OVER IN ENGLAND?

NOTHING *MUCH...* JUST TRYING TO SAVE THE *FREE WORLD...*

...AND I NEED A FEW *GOOD* MEN TO HELP ME MAKE THAT *HAPPEN.*

MEN WHO KNOW HOW TO *PARACHUTE,* MEN WHO KNOW HOW TO *HANDLE* THEMSELVES...

...MEN *LOYAL* TO THE U.S. OF A.

SOUND LIKE ANYONE YOU *KNOW?*

THAT SOUNDS LIKE *US,* SIR...BUT WE'RE *NOT* IN THE SERVICE.

THAT'S WHY I NEED YOU.

WE NEED *PLAUSIBLE DENIABILITY* IF THIS GOES BELLY UP.

SO WHAT EXACTLY *IS* THIS JOB?

SEEMS THERE'S A *NAZI SCIENTIST* WHO WANTS TO *DEFECT* TO AMERICA...

THE NIGHT THE FLAMING MAN ESCAPED HIS CONFINEMENT WAS ONE FEW IN THE CITY WOULD EVER FORGET.

BUT IT WAS JUST THE FIRST OF MANY UNFORGETTABLE NIGHTS SURROUNDING THE HUMAN TORCH.

DANGER
HIGH VOLTAGE
KEEP OUT

WE LATER LEARNED PROFESSOR HORTON HAD BEEN COMMUNICATING WITH HIS CREATION WHILE HE WAS ENTOMBED...

...TEACHING HIM ABOUT OUR WORLD, OUR HISTORY...

BUT NOW THE SYNTHETIC MAN WANTED TO EXPERIENCE IT FOR HIMSELF.

HE WANTED AN END TO HIS SOLITARY CONFINEMENT.

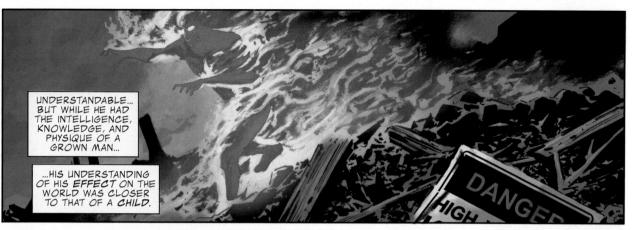

UNDERSTANDABLE... BUT WHILE HE HAD THE INTELLIGENCE, KNOWLEDGE, AND PHYSIQUE OF A GROWN MAN...

...HIS UNDERSTANDING OF HIS *EFFECT* ON THE WORLD WAS CLOSER TO THAT OF A *CHILD*.

AND HIS ABILITY TO CONTROL HIS *FLAMES* WAS, AT THAT POINT, TRAGICALLY *NONEXISTENT*.

NO! NO! **STAY BACK!**

KEEP AWAY FROM ME!

THE HORROR THAT RAN THROUGH HIS MIND AS THE CITY *BURNED* AT HIS TOUCH...

KEEP BACK!

...IS SOMETHING *FEW* LIVING CREATURES COULD COMPREHEND.

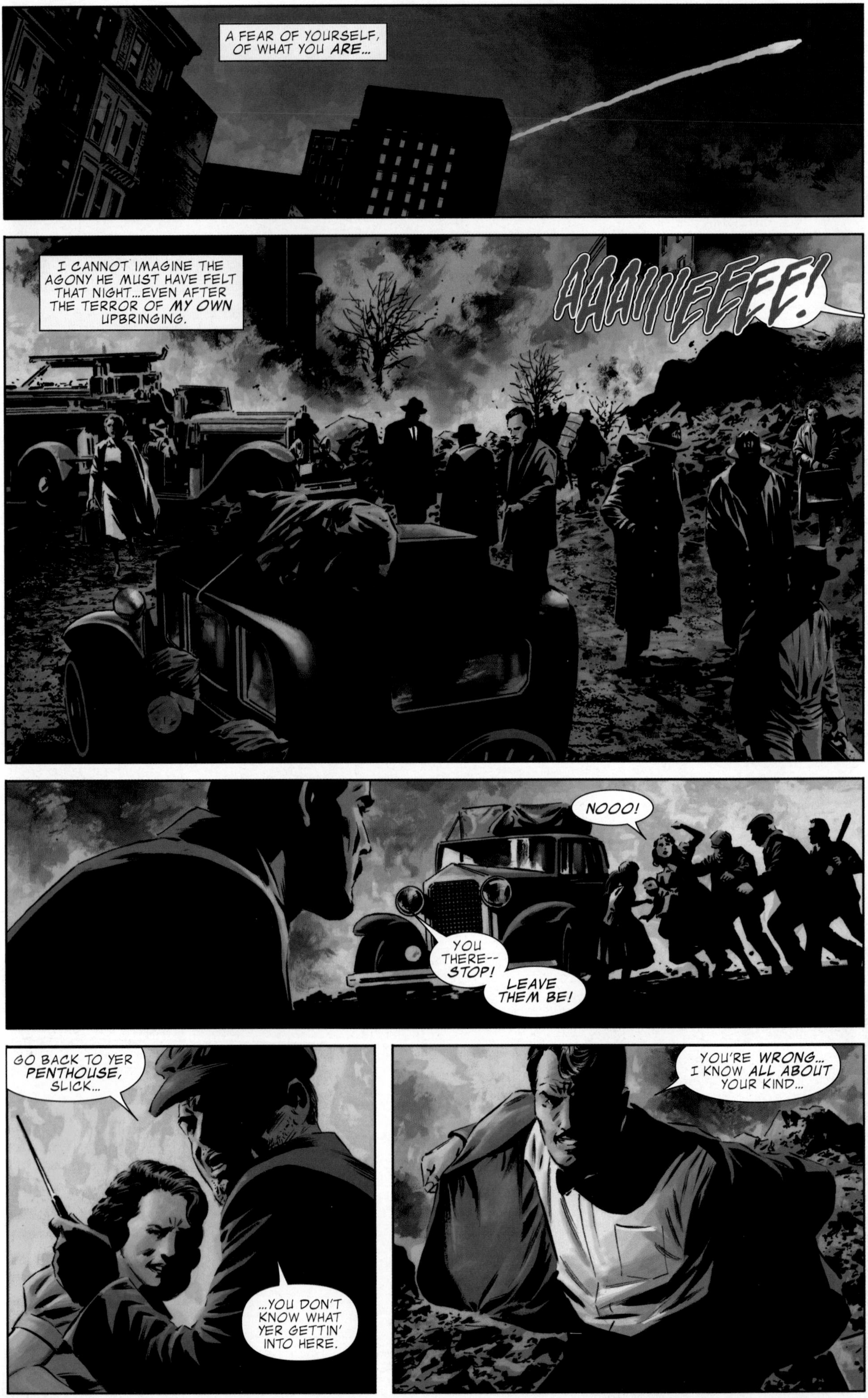
A FEAR OF YOURSELF, OF WHAT YOU ARE...
I CANNOT IMAGINE THE AGONY HE MUST HAVE FELT THAT NIGHT...EVEN AFTER THE TERROR OF MY OWN UPBRINGING.
AAAIIIEEEE!
NOOO!
YOU THERE-- STOP!
LEAVE THEM BE!
GO BACK TO YER PENTHOUSE, SLICK...
...YOU DON'T KNOW WHAT YER GETTIN' INTO HERE.
YOU'RE WRONG... I KNOW ALL ABOUT YOUR KIND...

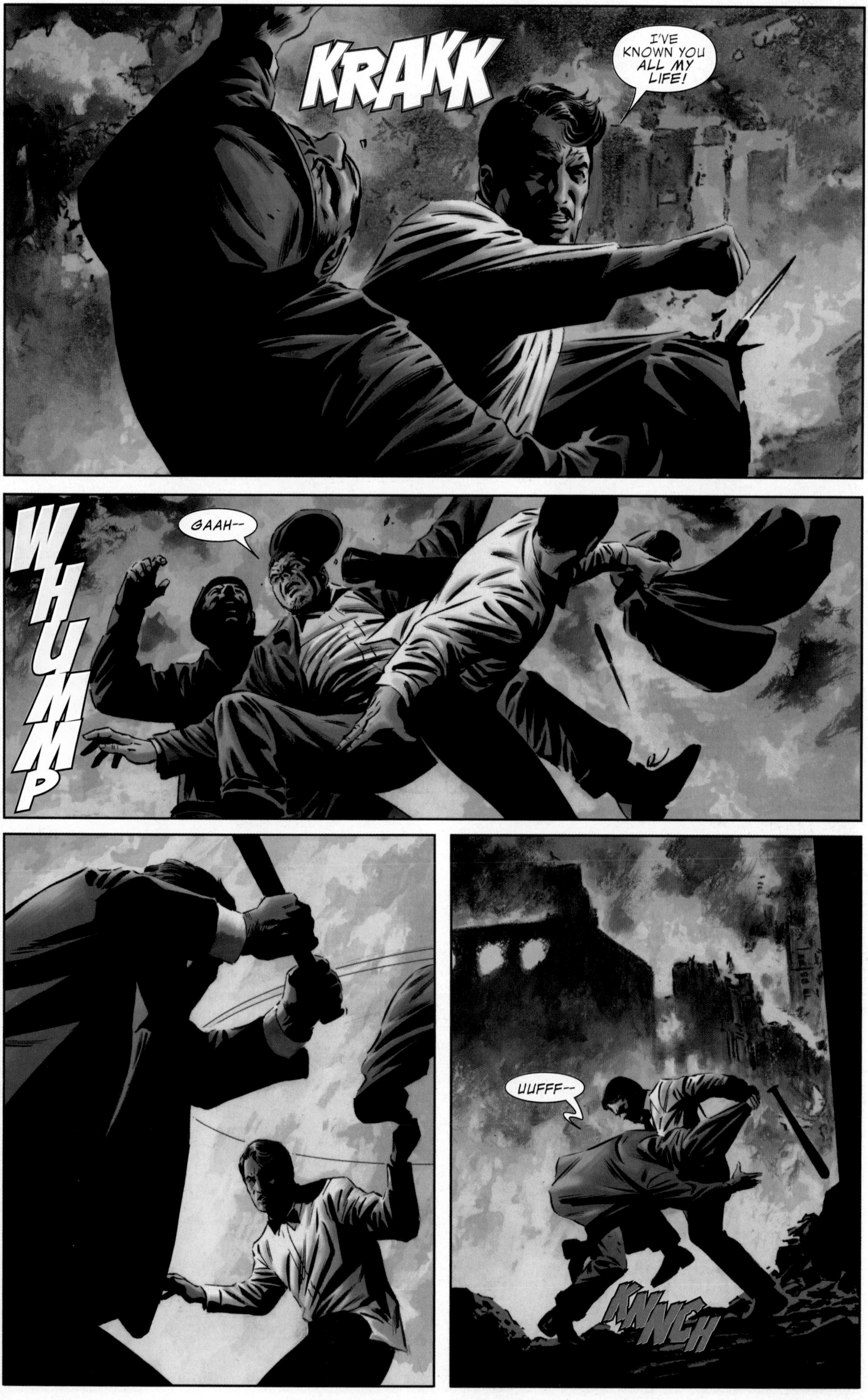
KRAKK
I'VE KNOWN YOU ALL MY LIFE!
WHUMMP
GAAH--
UUFFF--
KNNCH

SMAK

MA'AM...YOU'RE GOING TO WANT TO *AVOID* THE MAIN STREETS...

THE *FIRE TRUCKS* ARE CLOGGING THEM.

THEY'RE LOOTING...

...ALL THIS INSANITY... AND MEN ARE LOOTING...

YES... PEOPLE ARE *DISAPPOINTINGLY* PREDICTABLE, AREN'T THEY?

I DID WHAT I COULD THAT NIGHT TO PROTECT MY ADOPTED HOME.

I THOUGHT OF OLD MATT HAWK AND THE STORIES HE'D TOLD ME SO MANY TIMES....

HOW HE SAID IT WOULD ALL BEGIN HERE, IN NEW YORK CITY.

WAS THIS THE BEGINNING?

I WONDERED IF HE KNEW THAT IT WOULD BEGIN IN FLAMES AND DESTRUCTION...

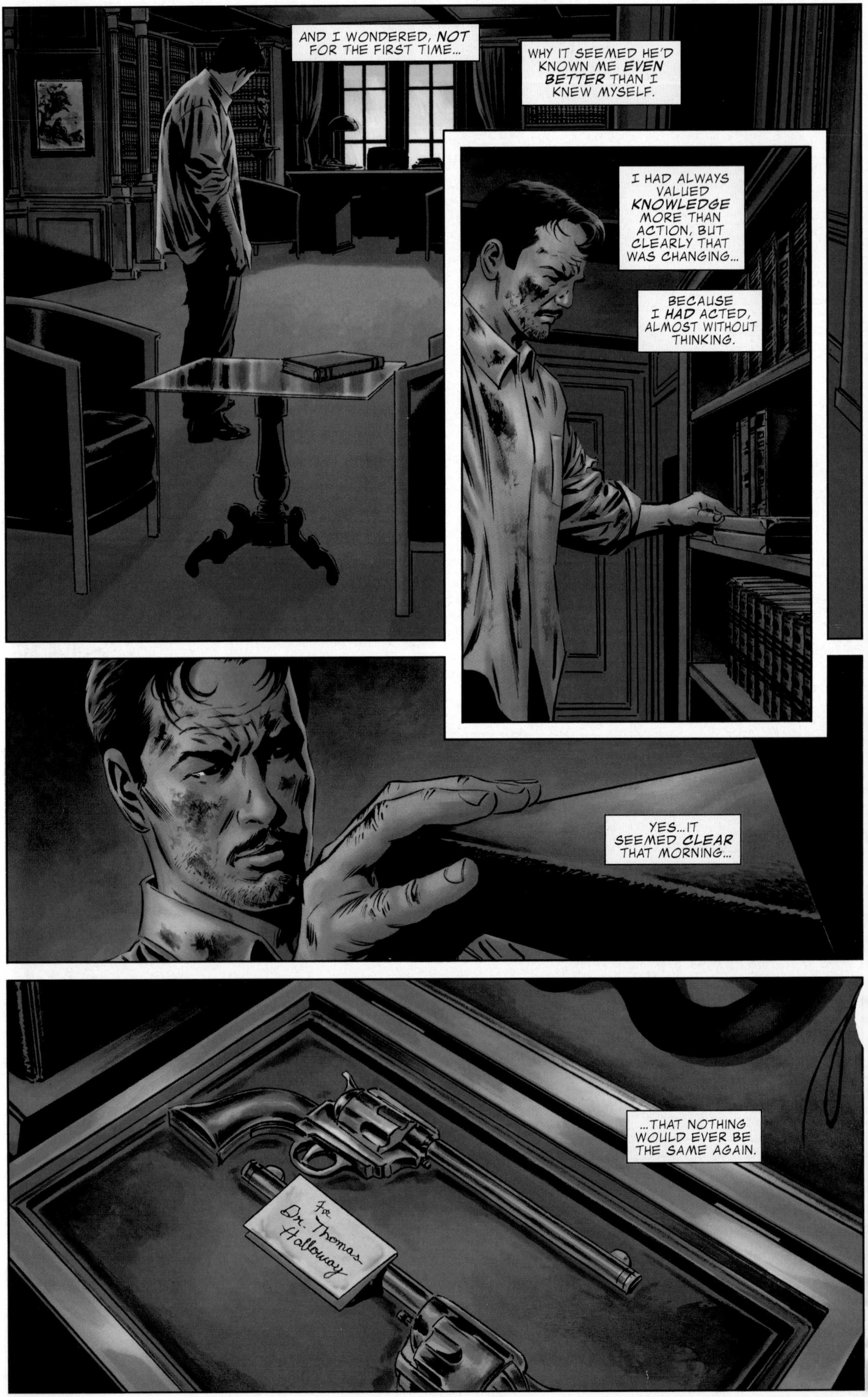
AND I WONDERED, NOT FOR THE FIRST TIME...
WHY IT SEEMED HE'D KNOWN ME EVEN BETTER THAN I KNEW MYSELF.
I HAD ALWAYS VALUED KNOWLEDGE MORE THAN ACTION, BUT CLEARLY THAT WAS CHANGING...
BECAUSE I HAD ACTED, ALMOST WITHOUT THINKING.
YES...IT SEEMED CLEAR THAT MORNING...
...THAT NOTHING WOULD EVER BE THE SAME AGAIN.
For Dr. Thomas Halloway

The Marvels Project # 2 Cover by Steve Epting

PART TWO

THE EARLY DAYS OF 1940 WERE A STRANGE TIME IN NEW YORK CITY.

AS WINTER CLUNG TO THE STREETS, THINGS WERE CHANGING.

MAYBE IT WAS BECAUSE OF THE CONTINUING PRESS COVERAGE OF THE HUMAN TORCH, AS THEY NOW CALLED HIM...

...STILL MISSING, OUT THERE... SOMEWHERE.

DAILY BUGLE
HUMAN TORCH SIGHTING IN YONKERS

OR MAYBE IT WAS JUST SOMETHING IN THE COLD NIGHT AIR THAT DROVE PEOPLE LIKE ME TO PUT ON MASKS...

...AND STALK THE NIGHT.

BECAUSE WE COULDN'T KNOW ABOUT THE *SECRET STRUGGLE* OUR GOVERNMENT AND *OTHERS* WERE ENGAGED IN...

‹SO THEY'VE BROUGHT *THIS ONE* OUT OF STORAGE AGAIN, HAVE THEY, HANS?›

‹OH...YOU *KNOW* OF HIM?›

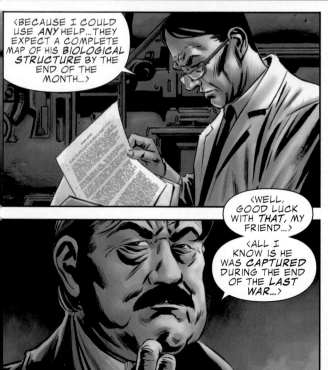

‹BECAUSE I COULD USE *ANY* HELP...THEY EXPECT A COMPLETE MAP OF HIS *BIOLOGICAL STRUCTURE* BY THE END OF THE MONTH...›

‹WELL, GOOD LUCK WITH *THAT*, MY FRIEND...›

‹ALL I KNOW IS HE WAS *CAPTURED* DURING THE END OF THE *LAST* WAR...›

‹ACCORDING TO *REPORTS*, HIS SKIN APPEARED TO BE *BULLETPROOF*...AND HE EXHIBITED *EXTRA-NORMAL* STRENGTH ON THE BATTLEFIELD.›

‹ALL OF MY EXAMINATIONS OF THIS *PRIVATE JOHN STEELE,* THOUGH...THEY PROVED *FRUITLESS...*›

‹HE APPEARS TO BE A COMPLETE AND UTTER *ANOMALY,* I'M AFRAID.›

‹PERHAPS YOU SHOULD SIMPLY *WAKE HIM UP* AND *ASK* HOW HE GOT THAT WAY, EH, HANS?›

‹EHH...I THINK *NOT,* ERSKINE.›

‹A JOKE, OLD FRIEND... JUST A JOKE.›

‹SO, YOU'RE OFF TO PRESENT YOUR *FINDINGS* TO *HERR HIMMLER* IN PERSON?›

‹YES, HE'S MEETING WITH FRIENDLY OFFICIALS IN LUXEMBOURG FOR A FEW DAYS, SO OFF I GO...›

‹SAFE TRAVEL, ABRAHAM.›

‹GOODBYE, HANS...›

"THE CONVOY TRANSPORTING *PROFESSOR ERSKINE* WILL HIT THE *EXTRACTION POINT* NEAR LUXEMBOURG AT APPROXIMATELY 0940 HOURS..."

"THIS IS OUR BEST SHOT *AND* THE CLOSEST HE'S BEEN TO THE *NAZI BORDER* SINCE HE CONTACTED US..."

YOU *POSITIVE* YOU'RE READY FOR THIS, FURY? BECAUSE WE AREN'T LIKELY TO GET ANOTHER CHANCE.

SURE, LIEUTENANT SAWYER...ME AND RED WERE *BORN* READY.

JUST MAKE SURE YOU AND THESE *SKY DEVILS* ARE WAITIN' WHEN WE NEED YOU...

...AND LET *US* DO THE HEAVY LIFTING!

WAHHOO!

FRIGGIN' YAHOOS...

WHICH CAR DID SAWYER SAY THE PROFESSOR WOULD BE IN?

ONE IN THE MIDDLE... THE OTHERS ARE HIS GUARDS.

I'LL TAKE OUT THE REAR CAR FIRST...

YOU FLATTEN THE TIRES ON THE PROF'S CAR... SO WE DON'T GO CHASIN' 'IM HALFWAY TO FRANCE.

NO PROBLEM, BUDDY...

...LIKE FISH IN A BARREL...

RIGHT... LET'S DO THIS.

THE CLASSIFIED REPORT ON THE *EXTRACTION* OF PROFESSOR ABRAHAM ERSKINE FROM BEHIND ENEMY LINES IS FULL OF HOLES.

REDACTED BITS, SOME NAMES WITHHELD.

BUT MANY THINGS ARE CLEAR IN THAT REPORT.

AMONG THEM, THAT *RED HARGROVE* AND *NICK FURY*, TWO INDEPENDENT SPECIAL OPERATIVES, PERFORMED BRAVELY AND *SWIFTLY*...

...THE ENTIRE ASSAULT LASTING UNDER *TWO* MINUTES.

AND IT *CANNOT* BE OVERSTATED HOW ENORMOUS THE LOSS OF ERSKINE WAS TO THE NAZI WAR EFFORT.

IT'S BEEN SAID THAT BECAUSE HE WAS TAKEN SO CLOSE TO THE *BORDER*...

...THAT THIS DEFECTION *MAY* HAVE HASTENED THE NAZI INVASION OF LUXEMBOURG, FRANCE AND BELGIUM.

...MEIN GOTT...

PROFESSOR ERSKINE?

ABRAHAM ERSKINE?

YES... YES, THAT IS I...

GOOD. YOU CAN RELAX NOW, PROFESSOR...

UNCLE SAM SENT US.

SWORDFISH ONE TO DEVIL'S HAMMER...WE ARE GO FOR *PICK-UP*...

WHEN I WAS DESIGNING MY DISGUISE, I WANTED TO ASSURE PEOPLE THE MASK DIDN'T MEAN I WAS A *THIEF* OR A *MURDERER*.

BUT I WONDERED HOW.

THEN I REMEMBERED WHAT THE CONVICTS USED TO CALL ME, GROWING UP IN MY FATHER'S PRISON.

YOU SEE, I ONCE *STOPPED* THE STATE FROM EXECUTING A *FALSELY ACCUSED* MURDERER THERE.

I PROVED HIS INNOCENCE *BASED ONLY ON HIS CASE FILE.* FATHER WAS DULY IMPRESSED.

I WAS JUST A *CHILD* THEN, ONLY 14 YEARS OLD, BUT ALREADY THE *CURRICULUM* HE HAD *FORCED* ON ME WAS HAVING AN EFFECT.

IN FACT, I FANCIED MYSELF A YOUNG *SHERLOCK HOLMES*...

...BUT THE CONS HAD ANOTHER NAME FOR ME...ONE I DIDN'T LIKE *SO WELL* BACK THEN...

...BUT WHICH FELT *APPROPRIATE* NOW...

HEY, MASKED MAN...WHATTA WE CALL YOU?

THE ANGEL...

...YOU CAN CALL ME *THE ANGEL.*

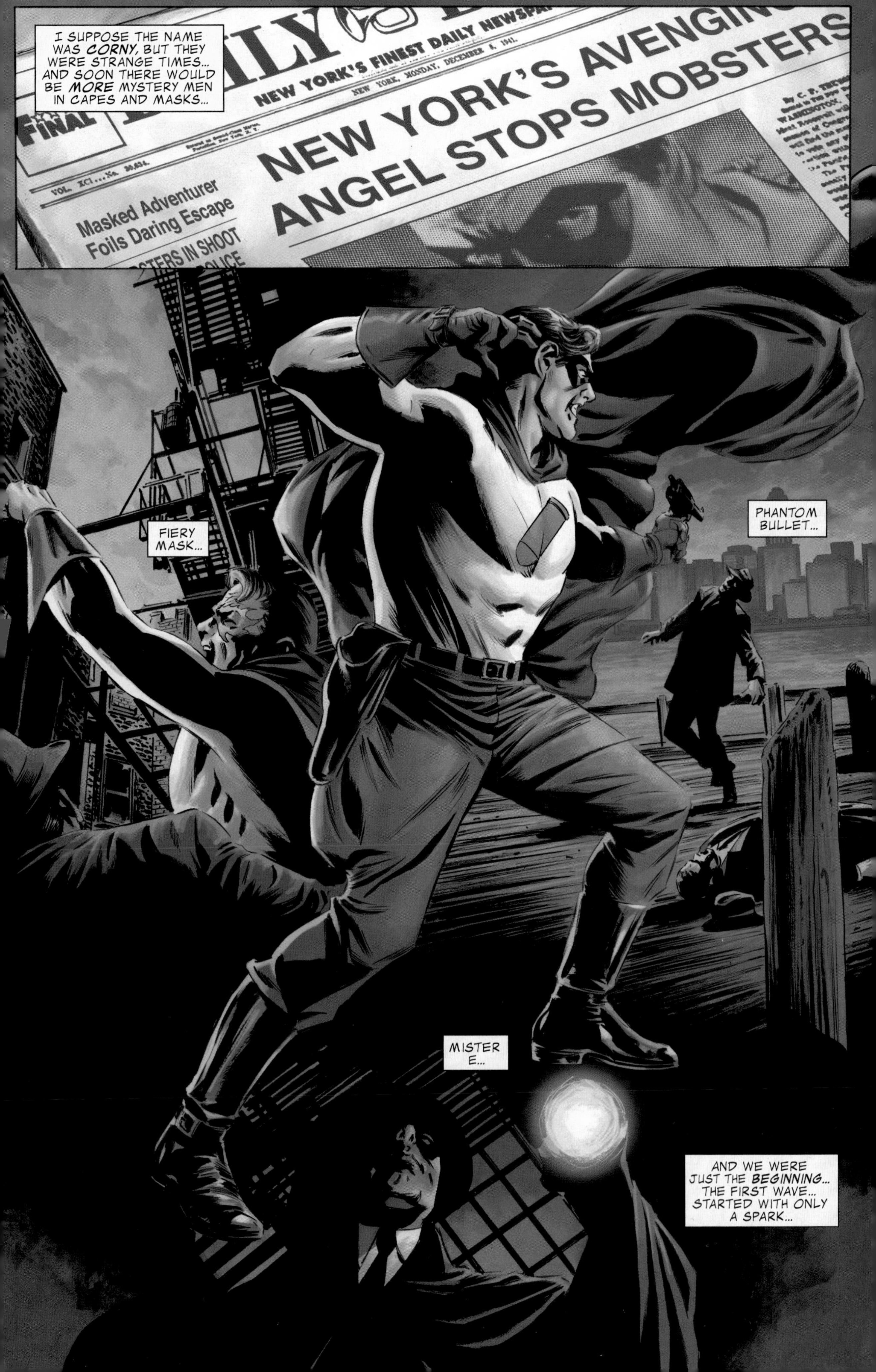
I SUPPOSE THE NAME WAS CORNY, BUT THEY WERE STRANGE TIMES... AND SOON THERE WOULD BE MORE MYSTERY MEN IN CAPES AND MASKS...
NEW YORK'S FINEST DAILY NEWSPA
FINAL
NEW YORK'S AVENGIN
ANGEL STOPS MOBSTERS
Masked Adventurer
Foils Daring Escape
FIERY MASK...
PHANTOM BULLET...
MISTER E...
AND WE WERE JUST THE BEGINNING... THE FIRST WAVE... STARTED WITH ONLY A SPARK...

...BUT NONE OF US KNEW YET WHAT HAD *BECOME* OF THAT SPARK.

I WOULD FIND OUT LATER THAT THE HUMAN TORCH WAS HIDING *FAR* FROM THE CITY...LEARNING TO CONTROL HIS FLAMES...

...AND TRYING TO FIGURE OUT EXACTLY *WHAT* HE WAS.

THOSE WERE LONELY MONTHS FOR HIM, BUT AS HIS *MATURITY* GREW...

...HE KNEW THAT HE FELT LIKE A *MAN*, NOT A *MONSTER*.

THAT HE HAD THE SAME DESIRES AND *FEARS* AS ANY NORMAL MAN...

C'MON, JIMMIE! YOU GOTTA BELIEVE ME!

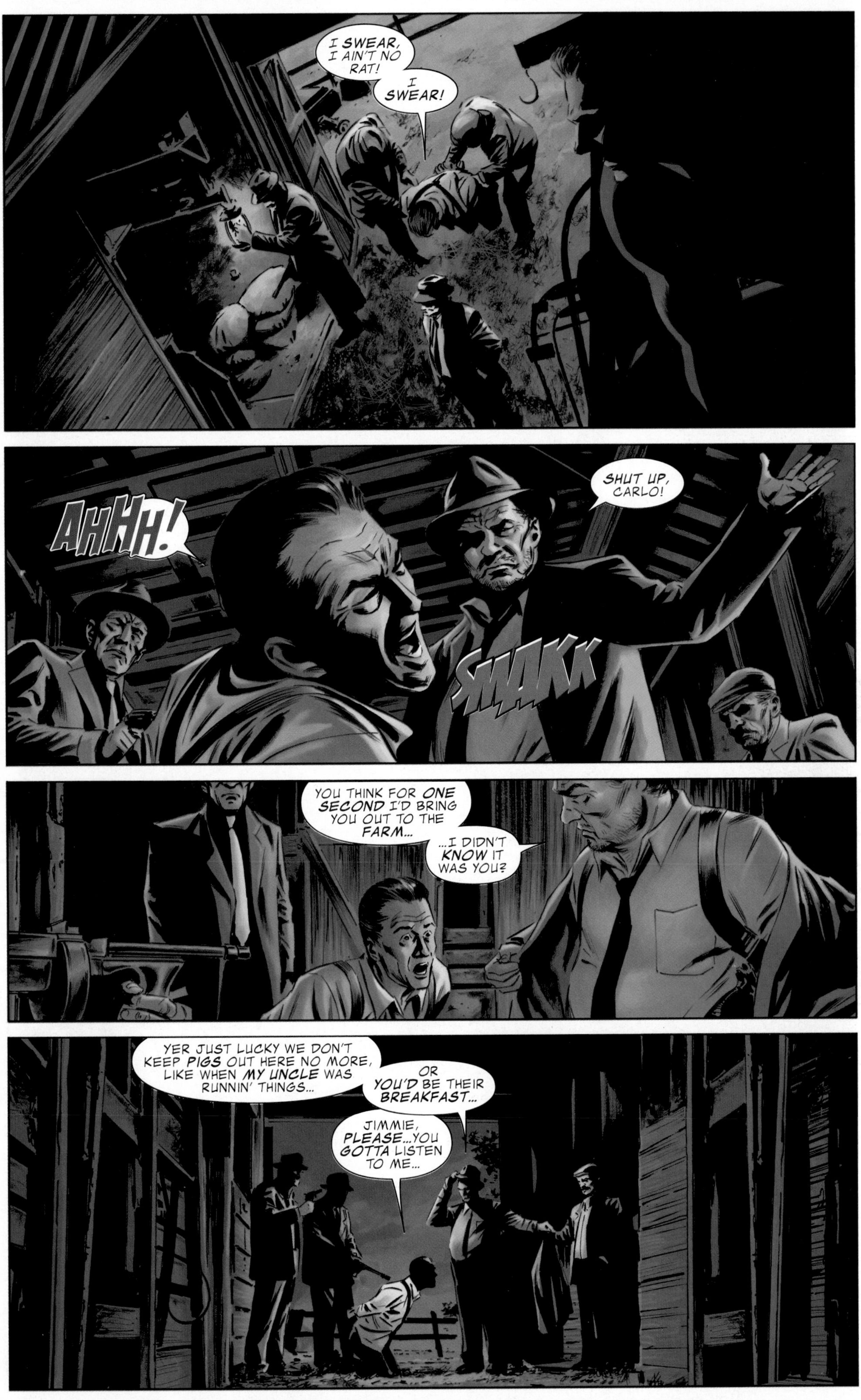
I SWEAR, I AIN'T NO RAT!
I SWEAR!
AHHH!
SHUT UP, CARLO!
SMAKK
YOU THINK FOR ONE SECOND I'D BRING YOU OUT TO THE FARM...
...I DIDN'T KNOW IT WAS YOU?
YER JUST LUCKY WE DON'T KEEP PIGS OUT HERE NO MORE, LIKE WHEN MY UNCLE WAS RUNNIN' THINGS...
OR YOU'D BE THEIR BREAKFAST...
JIMMIE, PLEASE...YOU GOTTA LISTEN TO ME...

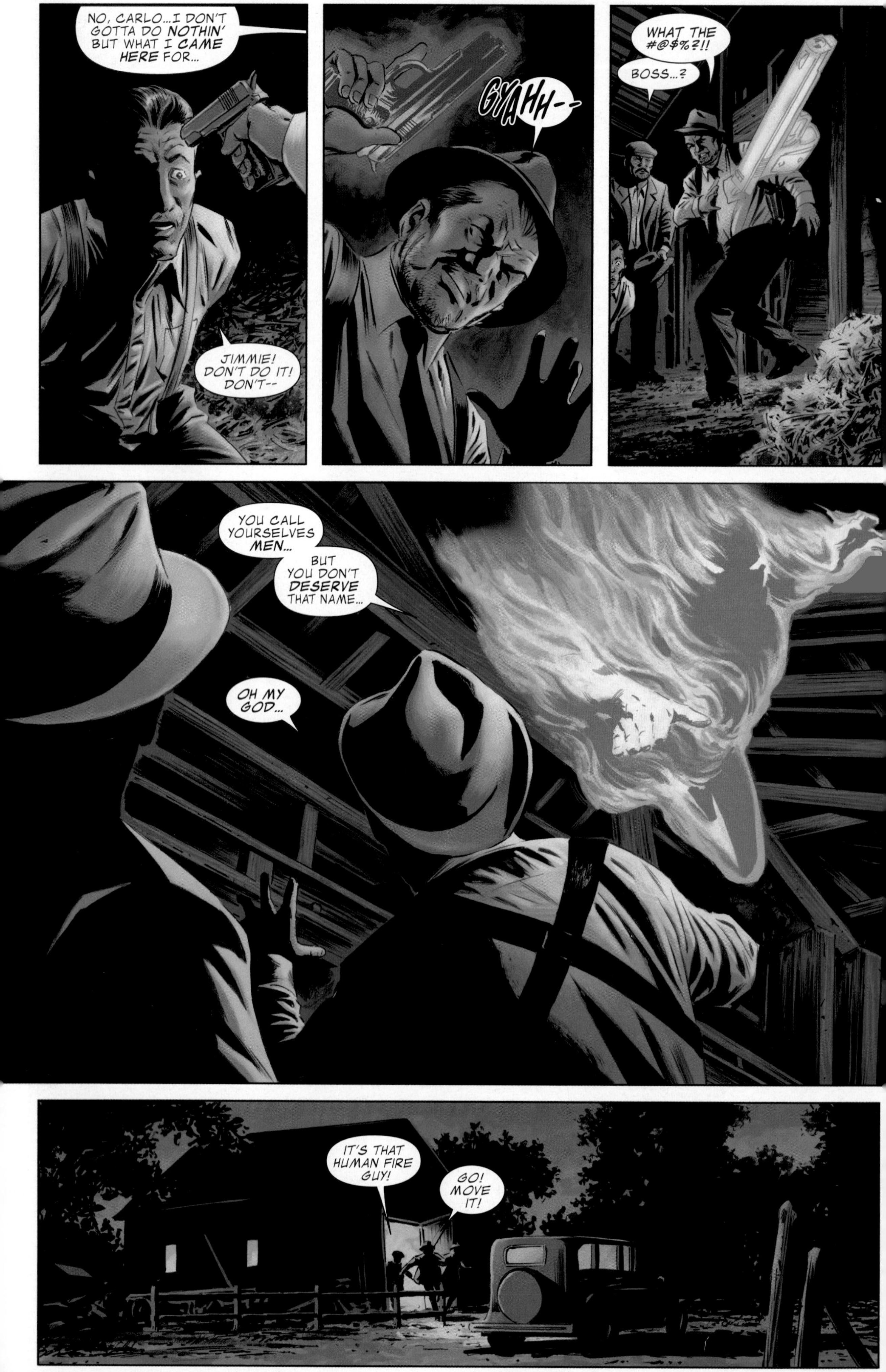
NO, CARLO...I DON'T GOTTA DO NOTHIN' BUT WHAT I CAME HERE FOR...
JIMMIE! DON'T DO IT! DON'T--
GYAHH--
WHAT THE #@$%?!!
BOSS...?
YOU CALL YOURSELVES MEN...
BUT YOU DON'T DESERVE THAT NAME...
OH MY GOD...
IT'S THAT HUMAN FIRE GUY!
GO! MOVE IT!

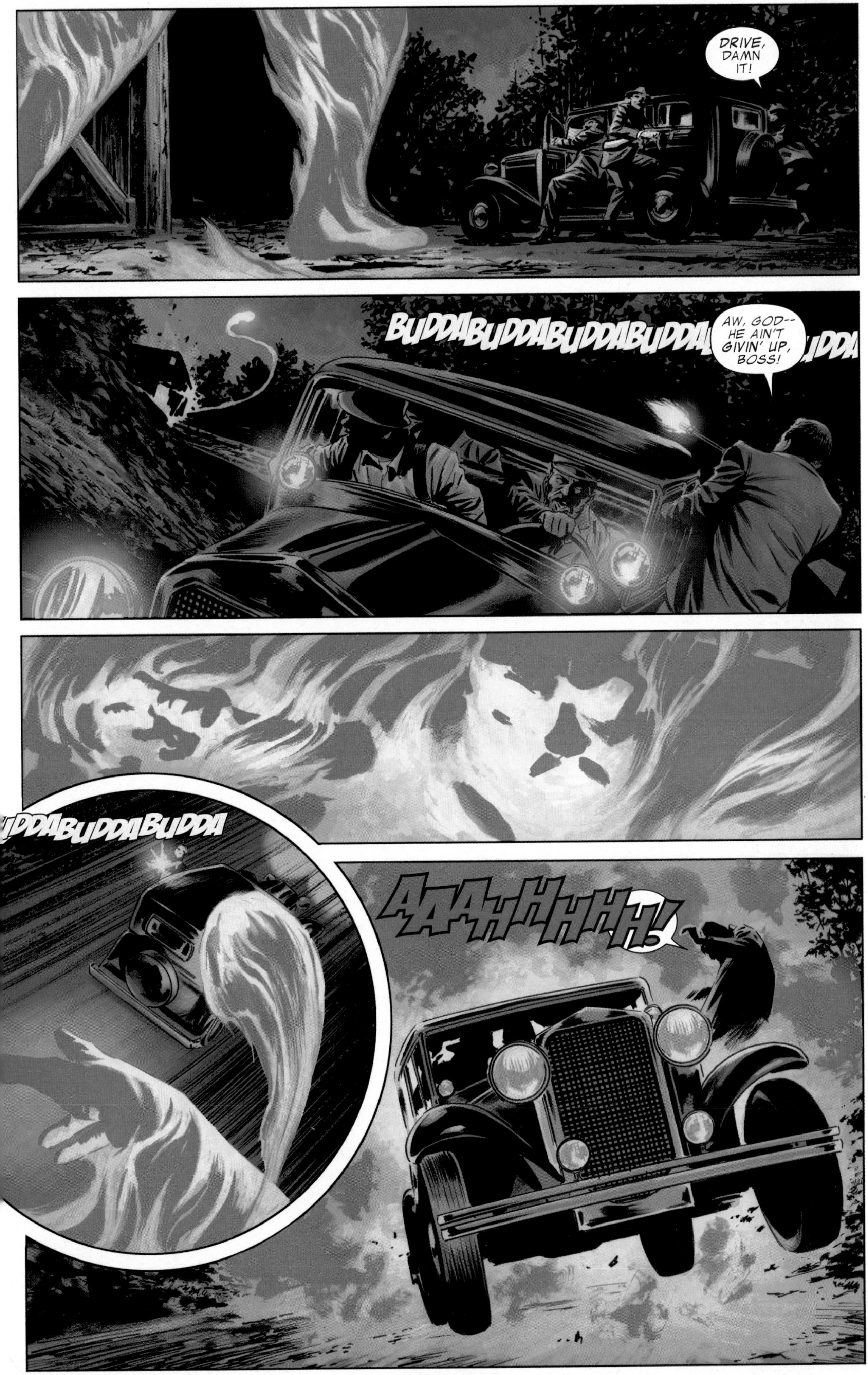
DRIVE, DAMN IT!
BUDDABUDDABUDDABUDDA
AW, GOD-- HE AIN'T GIVIN' UP, BOSS!
UDDA
UDDABUDDABUDDA
AAAHHHHH!

HEY, TAKE IT *EASY*, PAL... I'M NOT WITH *THEM*...

IS THAT *SO?*

YEAH... I... I WORK FOR THE *COPS*...

Y'KNOW... I'M LIKE YOU...

...ONE OF THE *GOOD GUYS.*

BACK IN THE CITY, THE REST OF US GOOD GUYS WERE STARTING TO FEEL LIKE WE WERE MAKING A DIFFERENCE...

...AS WINTER TURNED TO SPRING, AND THE STREETS CAME TO LIFE AGAIN.

CROWDS LINED UP DAILY TO SEE *MONAKO THE GREAT* PERFORM IN TIMES SQUARE...

AND RUMOR WAS THAT MONAKO WAS A MYSTIC DETECTIVE IN HIS HOURS OFF-STAGE...

I'D SEEN HIS SHOW A FEW TIMES, AND I COULD EASILY BELIEVE IT.

BUT THOSE EARLY, INNOCENT DAYS, THEY DIDN'T LAST LONG...

HEY... I THINK I KNOW THIS GUY... WHAT'S HIS NAME?

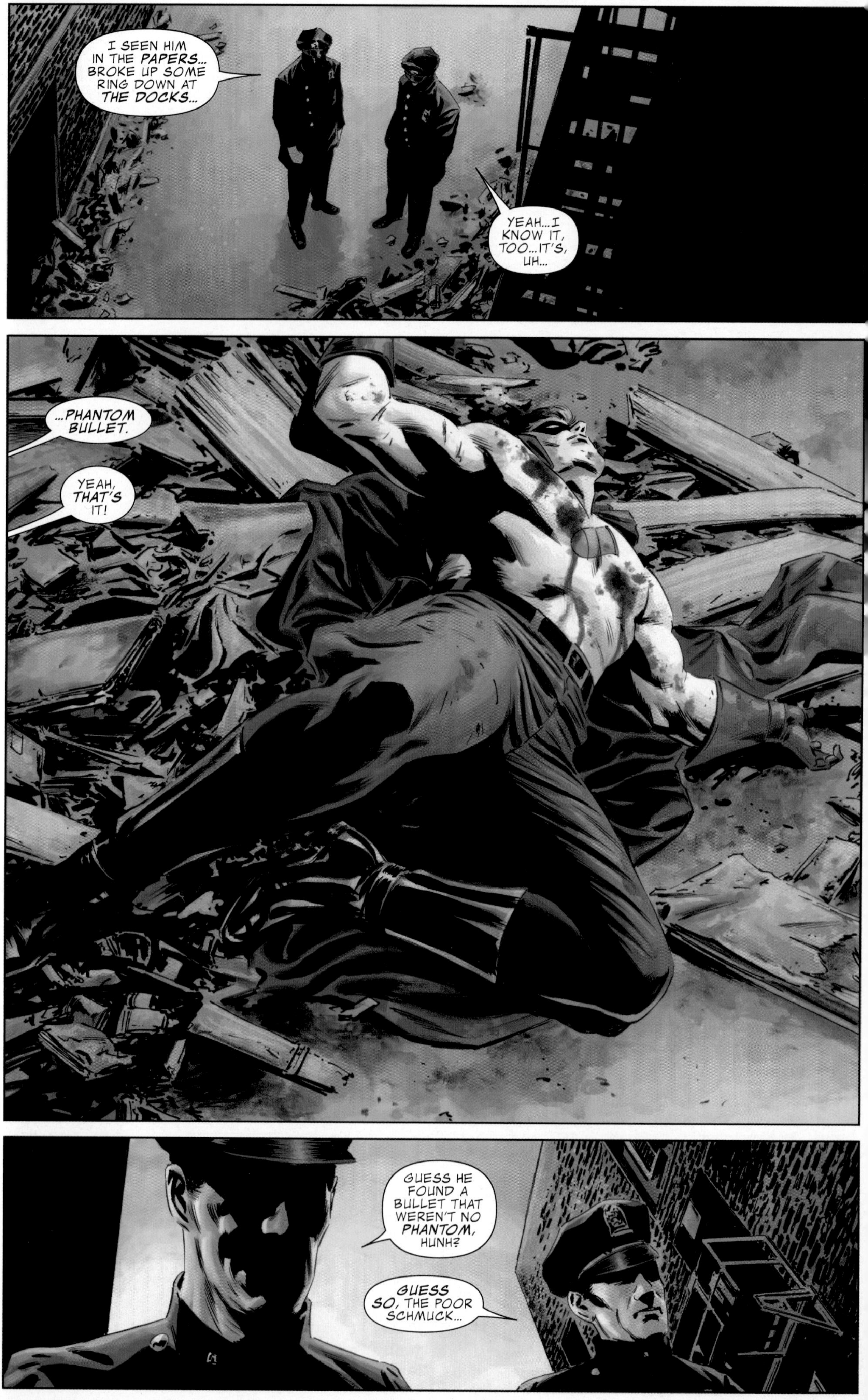
I SEEN HIM IN THE PAPERS... BROKE UP SOME RING DOWN AT THE DOCKS...
YEAH...I KNOW IT, TOO...IT'S, UH...
...PHANTOM BULLET.
YEAH, THAT'S IT!
GUESS HE FOUND A BULLET THAT WEREN'T NO PHANTOM, HUNH?
GUESS SO, THE POOR SCHMUCK...

ALMOST FEEL *SORRY* FOR HIM. RUNNIN' AROUND IN THAT OUTFIT WAS BAD ENOUGH...BUT *DYIN'* IN IT?

...THAT'S JUST PLAIN *EMBARRASSIN'*...

THE POLICE DIDN'T APPRECIATE US, ANY OF US.

AT BEST WE WERE AN *INSULT* TO THEM...

...AT WORST, WE WERE LIKE *THE TORCH*...A *HAZARD*.

THE PHANTOM BULLET, ONLY ACTIVE A FEW MONTHS, AND ALREADY STRUCK DOWN...LEFT IN THE GARBAGE.

I DIDN'T KNOW HIM, BUT IT HURT LIKE I'D LOST A BROTHER.

IF ONLY I'D KNOWN THAT DAY HOW MUCH MORE BLOODSHED THERE WAS TO COME...

‹...WE EXPECT YOU TO MONITOR THE SITUATION, IF YOU CAN, MAJOR KERFOOT.›

‹OF COURSE. WHATEVER THE FÜHRER WANTS FROM ME, I SHALL GIVE...›

‹ARE WE CERTAIN IT IS THE AMERICANS THAT HERR ERSKINE HAS DEFECTED TO? THAT HE IS COMING HERE?›

‹YOU MUST OPERATE UNDER THAT ASSUMPTION AT THIS POINT...›

‹REPORT BACK WHEN YOU HEAR MORE, KERFOOT, AND DON'T LET US DOWN...›

‹OF COURSE, COMMANDER...›

HEIL HITLER.

PROFESSOR HAMILTON, ARE YOU...?

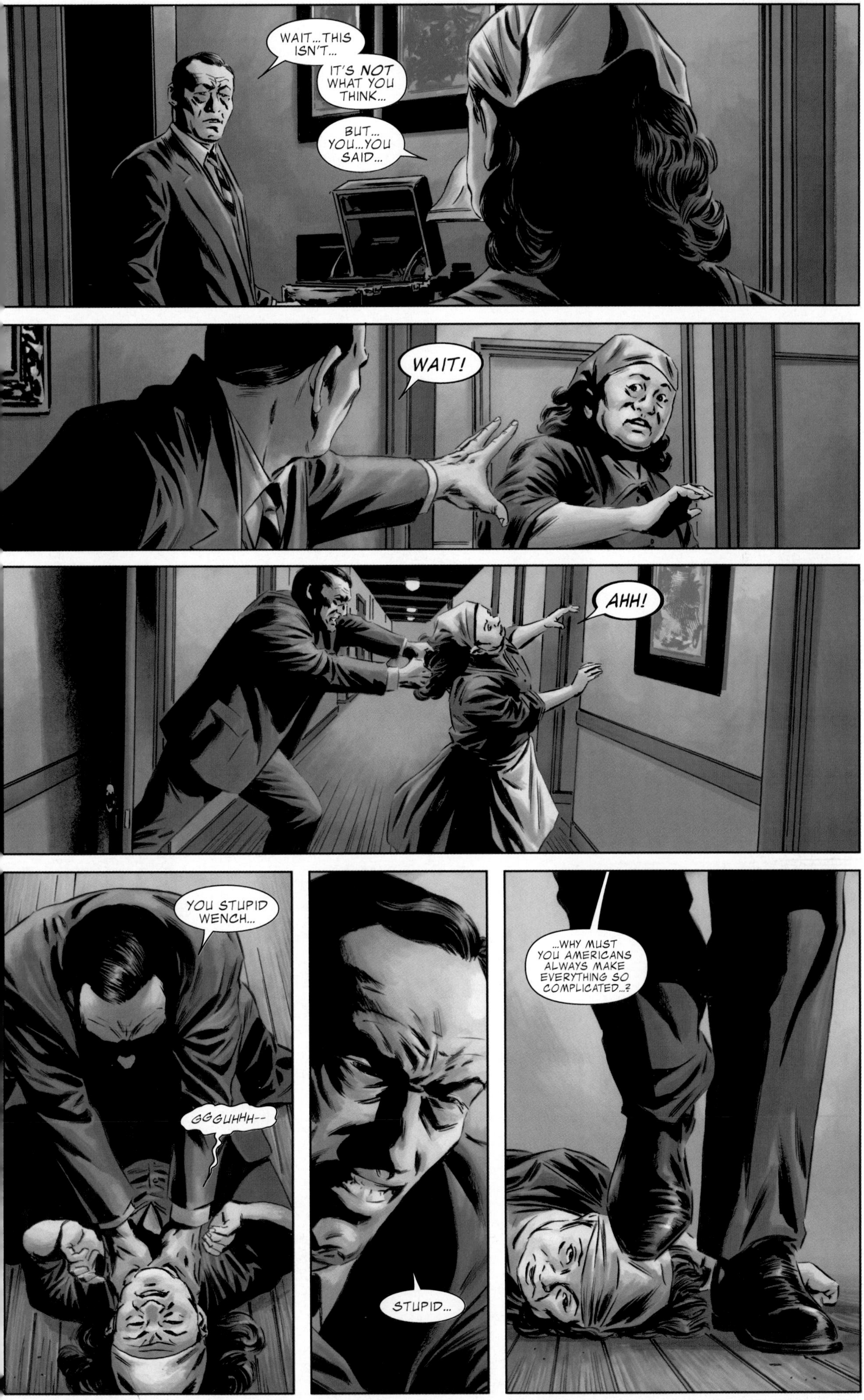
WAIT...THIS ISN'T...
IT'S NOT WHAT YOU THINK...
BUT... YOU...YOU SAID...
WAIT!
AHH!
YOU STUPID WENCH...
GGGUHHH--
STUPID...
...WHY MUST YOU AMERICANS ALWAYS MAKE EVERYTHING SO COMPLICATED...?

PHANTOM BULLET'S REAL NAME WAS *ALLAN LEWIS*, AND I FIT IN EASILY ENOUGH IN THE CROWD AT HIS FUNERAL.

BUT SEEING HIM UP-CLOSE AND UNMASKED, I WAS IN FOR A SHOCK...

ALLAN LEWIS WAS THE *REPORTER* FROM THE *DAILY BULLETIN* WHO HAD TAKEN MY PICTURE AND WRITTEN ABOUT MY EXPLOITS...

AND I'D READ HIS EARLIER ARTICLES, ABOUT THE HUNT FOR THE HUMAN TORCH.

AS THEY LOWERED HIS COFFIN INTO THE GROUND, I COULD FEEL ITS WEIGHT BEING LOWERED ONTO MY SHOULDERS.

I MADE A SILENT VOW TO BRING HIS KILLER TO JUSTICE.

AND ACROSS TOWN, ANOTHER HERO WAS FINDING HIS WAY TOWARDS JUSTICE...

...AND REDEMPTION.

CAN I *HELP YA'* WIT' SOMETHIN', KID?

YES...

...HOW DOES ONE GO ABOUT *JOINING* THE *POLICE FORCE*...?

The Marvels Project # 3 Cover by Steve Epting

PART THREE

SUMMER HIT NEW YORK IN 1940 ALMOST WITHOUT WARNING.

MAYBE AFTER THE EVENTS OF LAST WINTER AND THE POOR EXCUSE WE HAD FOR A SPRING, WE'D FORGOTTEN TO EXPECT IT.

GREENWICH VILLAGE, NEW YORK CITY.

BUT HERE IT WAS, REMINDING US THAT LIFE--AND DEATH-- MARCHED ON...

THE FERRET CONFIDENTIAL INVESTIGATIONS

NORMALLY, I WOULD LET THE POLICE HANDLE IT...

NONSENSE, MISS PORTNOY... POLICE MAKE MISSING PERSONS THEIR LOWEST PRIORITY...

IF THEY PRIORITIZE IT AT ALL, THAT IS.

THAT WAS THE IMPRESSION I WAS GETTING FROM THEM...

YOU SEE, IT'S BEEN OVER A MONTH SINCE MOTHER DISAPPEARED...

AND THE BEST THEY CAN SAY IS THAT SHE'S OLD AND MAY HAVE WANDERED OFF...

BUT MOTHER *WASN'T* OLD LIKE THAT...WASN'T *SENILE.* SHE STILL *CLEANED HOUSES* ALMOST DAILY...

AND SO YOU FEAR *FOUL PLAY?*

I'M AFRAID I *DO,* MISTER... UM...

IT'S QUITE *ALL RIGHT,* MADAM, EVERYONE CALLS ME *THE FERRET* THESE DAYS.

DON'T THEY, *NOSIE...?*

KKKRRIITT KKRIIT

AND YOU CAN REST *ASSURED,* IF THERE *HAS* BEEN ANY FOUL PLAY...NOSIE AND I WILL *ROOT IT OUT...*

THAT'S WHAT WE *DO.*

AND IN UPTOWN MANHATTAN...

PLEASE EXCUSE THE STATE OF THE *APARTMENT,* GENERAL...

...MY USUAL *MAID* SEEMS TO HAVE DECIDED EARTH IS *FLAT* AND FALLEN OFF THE SIDE... HEH HEH...

NONSENSE, PROFESSOR HAMILTON...

I LIVE IN THE *B.O.Q...* I'VE SEEN *FAR* WORSE.

CAN I OFFER YOU SOME *TEA*, GENERAL, OR...?

AFRAID THERE'S NOT A LOT OF TIME FOR PLEASANTRIES.

I'M ON *UNCLE SAM'S* TIME HERE.

YOU KNOW WE'VE BEEN VETTING YOUR *BACKGROUND* ALREADY FOR SOME OF OUR ROBOTICS PROJECTS...

I WASN'T SURE THOSE WERE STILL *ONGOING*...AFTER THAT "*HUMAN TORCH*" FIASCO...

I CAN'T COMMENT ON THAT, OF COURSE...

BUT THERE'S A *NEW PROJECT* STAFFING UP, AND WE'D LIKE YOU ONBOARD.

OF *COURSE*, GENERAL...*WHENEVER* YOU NEED, *WHATEVER* YOU NEED.

I LIVE TO SERVE MY *COUNTRY*...

GOOD TO HEAR...WE'LL NEED MORE *PATRIOTS* LIKE YOU SOON, HAMILTON...

CAN'T STAY OUT OF THIS DAMN WAR *FOREVER*, CAN WE?

NO... INDEED.

STILL A FREELANCING *YAHOO*, EH, FURY?!

LIEUTENANT *SAWYER?* THOUGHT YOU'D BE OVER IN THE STATES WITH THAT *KRAUT SCIENTIST* WE RESCUED...

NO SUCH *LUCK*, NICK...

KNOW WHAT THEY *SAY*...NO REST FOR THE WICKED.

BUT ERSKINE *IS* WORKING OUT FINE SO FAR.

IF WE COULD *ACKNOWLEDGE* YOUR ACTIONS THAT DAY, YOU AND RED'D BE WEARING *MEDALS* RIGHT NOW.

AH, MEDALS'RE FOR *PANSIES*...

RED AN' ME WERE JUST DOIN' WHAT *ANY* REAL AMERICAN WOULD DO...

STICKIN' A *THUMB* IN UNCLE ADOLF'S EYE.

HOW'D YOU LIKE TO PUT THE **WHOLE FIST** IN HIS EYE THIS TIME?

A **NEW** MISSION?

YEAH...WE FINALLY **PINPOINTED** SOME OF THE FACILITIES WHERE THE S.S. **MOVED** ERSKINE'S FELLOW **SCIENTISTS** AFTER HIS DEFECTION...

YEAH, THE OLD PROF HELPED US FIND THEM... HE'S SHARP AS HELL...

'BOUT FRIGGIN' TIME.

SO...WHAT SAY YOU AND RED AND THE **SKY DEVILS** GO FIND SOME HIDDEN NAZI FORTRESSES?

HIDING IN PLAIN SIGHT, ON THE OTHER HAND, WAS WORKING JUST FINE FOR THE *HUMAN TORCH*...

...OR *OFFICER HAMMOND,* AS HE WAS NOW KNOWN.

HE'D TAKEN THE JOB TO MAKE UP *(IN SOME SMALL WAY)* FOR THE DAMAGE HE'D DONE TO THE CITY.

AND PERHAPS TO *LEARN* WHAT IT MEANT TO BE ONE OF THE "GOOD GUYS."

BUT HE HADN'T EXPECTED IT WOULD AFFECT HIM SO QUICKLY...HUMANITY.

STOPPING CRIMINALS FROM *VICTIMIZING* THE WEAK AND ELDERLY...

...PROTECTING THE *INNOCENT.*

ESPECIALLY WITHOUT USING HIS POWERS.

IT FILLED HIM WITH A PRIDE HE'D *NEVER* EXPERIENCED, SEEING THE FACES OF THE CITIZENS AS HE WALKED HIS BEAT.

CREEZUS, *HAMMOND...* YER MAKIN' THE REST OF US *LOOK BAD.*

SAYS HERE YOU AIN'T EVEN TAKEN *A DAY OFF* SINCE YOU STARTED...

A DAY OFF? DO I HAVE TO?

YEAH, YOU HAVE'TA.

BUT...WHAT SHOULD I DO?

I *DUNNO,* SUPER-COP...DO WHAT *NORMAL* PEOPLE DO...

...GO TO 'CONEY ISLAND...

MY SUMMER WASN'T GOING AS WELL AS JIM HAMMOND'S WAS...

I WAS TRYING TO FULFILL MY VOW TO A FALLEN COMRADE-- *THE PHANTOM BULLET.*

HIS TERRITORY HAD BEEN THE *DOCKS,* WHICH HE HAD *ALSO* COVERED AS A REPORTER, NOT COINCIDENTALLY.

AND THE NEW YORK DOCKS IN 1940 WERE A FOG OF CORRUPTION, MOB VIOLENCE, AND SHADY CHARACTERS.

SO I FOUND MYSELF DOING *LESS* INVESTIGATING AND MORE...

...WELL, BEATING PEOPLE TO A *PULP.*

SKRASSH

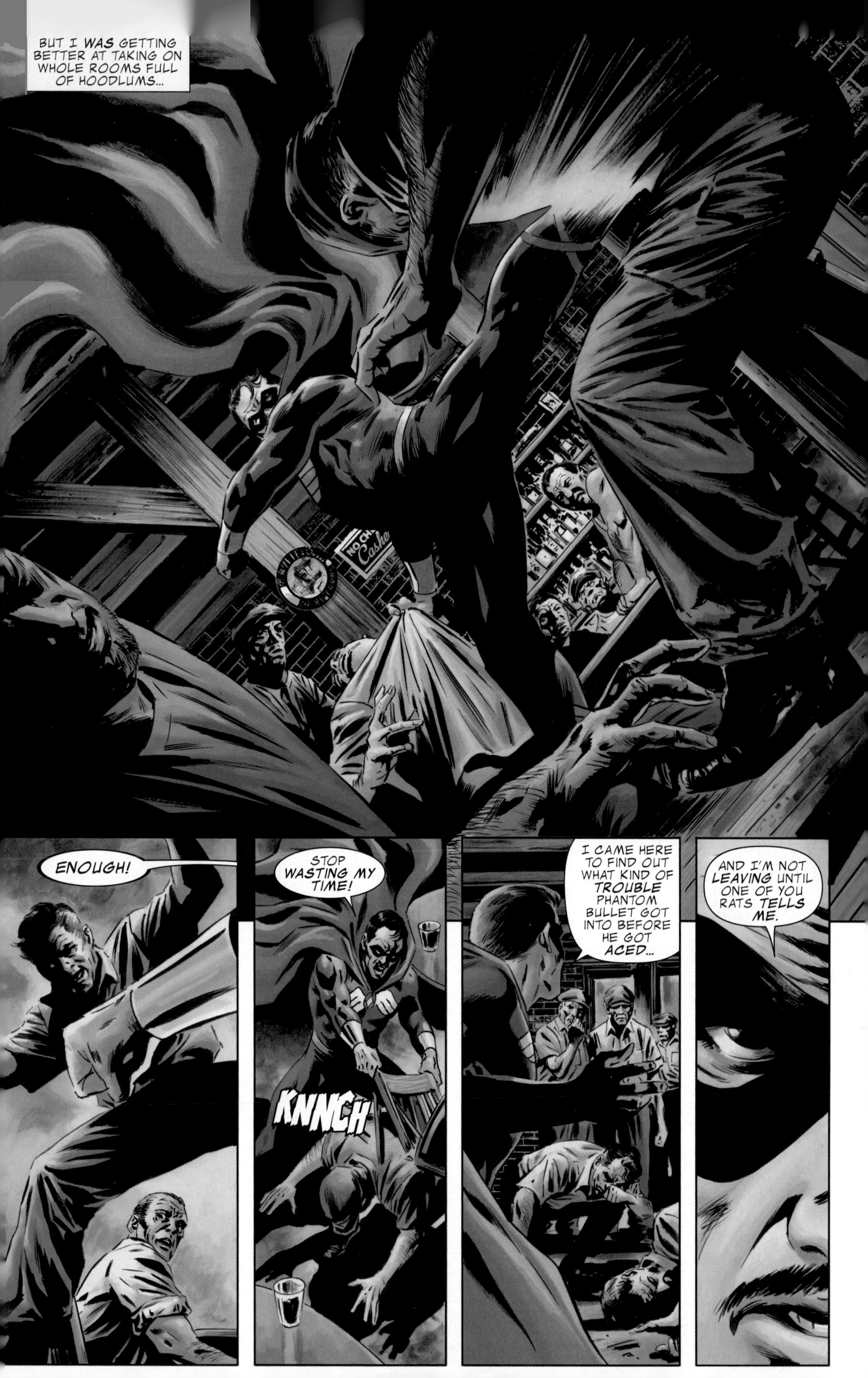
BUT I WAS GETTING BETTER AT TAKING ON WHOLE ROOMS FULL OF HOODLUMS...
ENOUGH!
STOP WASTING MY TIME!
KNNCH
I CAME HERE TO FIND OUT WHAT KIND OF TROUBLE PHANTOM BULLET GOT INTO BEFORE HE GOT ACED...
AND I'M NOT LEAVING UNTIL ONE OF YOU RATS TELLS ME.

LOOK...ANGEL... WE DON'T *KNOW*, I SWEAR...

DON'T GIVE ME *THAT*, JOSIE...

I KNOW HOW WORD *SPREADS* DOWN HERE...

YEAH, BUT... THAT *COSTUMED* FREAK...

NO OFFENSE...

HE WAS IN *EVERYBODY'S* BUSINESS...HOW SHOULD *WE* KNOW WHO HE *TICKED* OFF THE MOST?

GOOD POINT, BUT I'M GUESSING FOLKS DOWN HERE DON'T SIT ON *GRUDGES* FOR TOO LONG, DO THEY?

ONE THING *I* HEARD, A WEEK OR SO BEFORE HE *GOT* IT... HE BUSTED UP SOME KINDA *SMUGGLIN'* OPERATION...

SMUGGLING *WHAT*?

AIN'T SURE...*GUNS*, I THINK...BUT I HEARD MAYBE SOME *PEOPLE* WAS SNEAKIN' IN, TOO.

SEE? NOW WAS THAT SO *HARD*?

IT WAS A START, A DETAIL TO GO ON...AND I'D LEARNED LONG AGO THAT THE PATH TO TRUTH WAS OFTEN HIDDEN IN THE SMALL DETAILS.

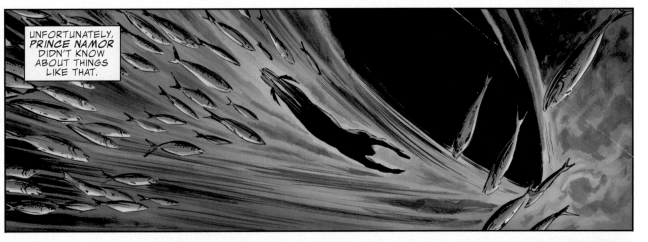

UNFORTUNATELY, *PRINCE NAMOR* DIDN'T KNOW ABOUT THINGS LIKE THAT.

FOR MONTHS NOW, HE'D SEEN ONLY THE *LARGER* DETAILS...

...THE DEATH OF HIS PEOPLE...THE DESTRUCTION OF HIS CITY BENEATH THE SEA...

AND IN HIS EYES, ALL SURFACE-DWELLERS WERE ONE PEOPLE.

SO WHEN HE FOLLOWED A MERCHANT SHIP TOWARD NEW YORK'S SHORES...

...WHAT HE SAW **ENRAGED** HIM.

HERE WERE HAPPY CHILDREN AND PARENTS...

HERE WERE RIDES AND BRIGHT LIGHTS AND LOUD NOISES...

THE SURFACE WORLD, **CELEBRATING**...WHILE HIS KINGDOM FELL TO RUIN AND HIS PEOPLE SUFFERED... IT WAS MORE THAN HE COULD STAND.

RRRAAAAA!

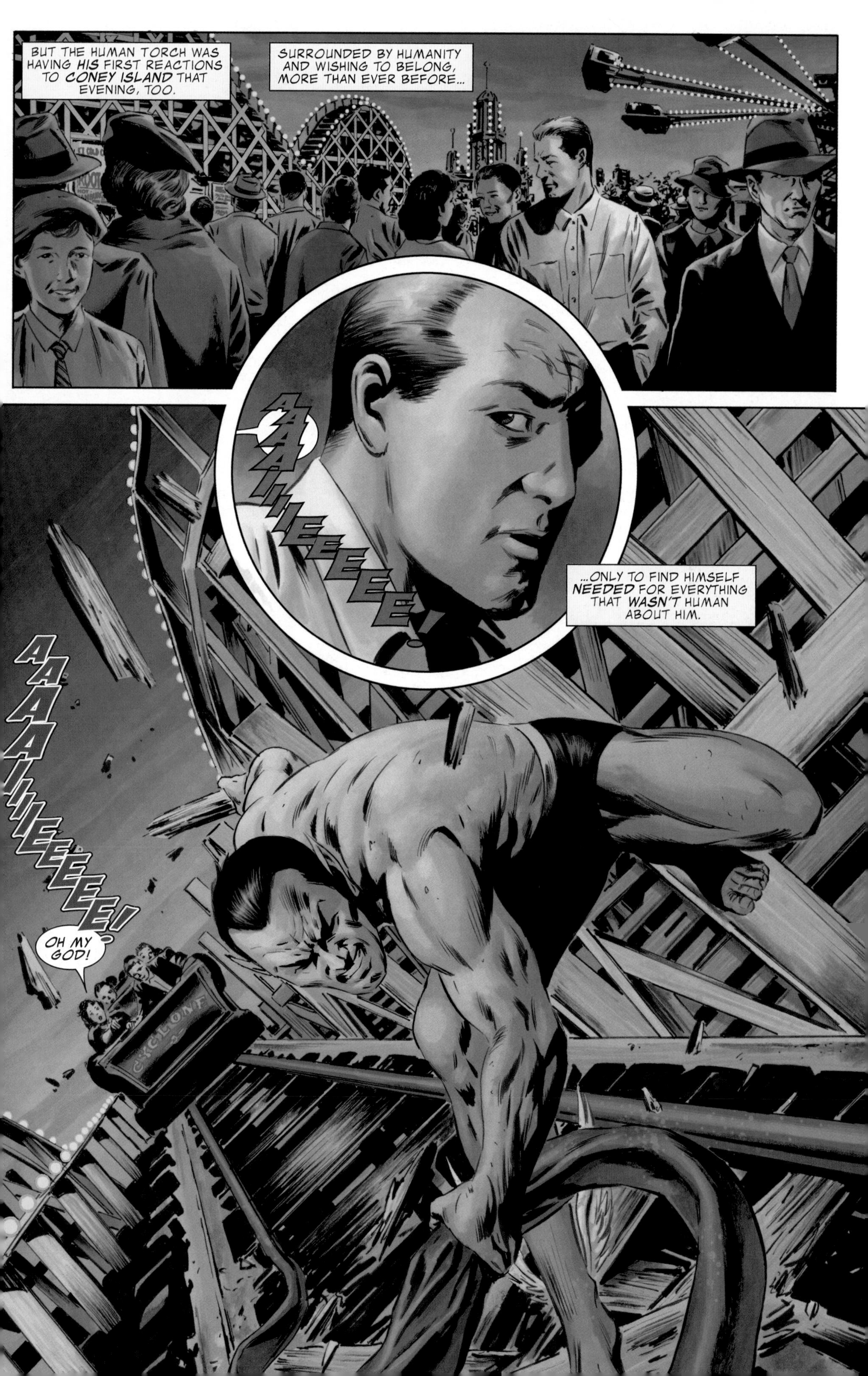
BUT THE HUMAN TORCH WAS HAVING HIS FIRST REACTIONS TO CONEY ISLAND THAT EVENING, TOO.
SURROUNDED BY HUMANITY AND WISHING TO BELONG, MORE THAN EVER BEFORE...
AAAIIIIEEEEEEE!
...ONLY TO FIND HIMSELF NEEDED FOR EVERYTHING THAT WASN'T HUMAN ABOUT HIM.
AAAAAIIIIIEEEEEEE!
OH MY GOD!
CYCLONE

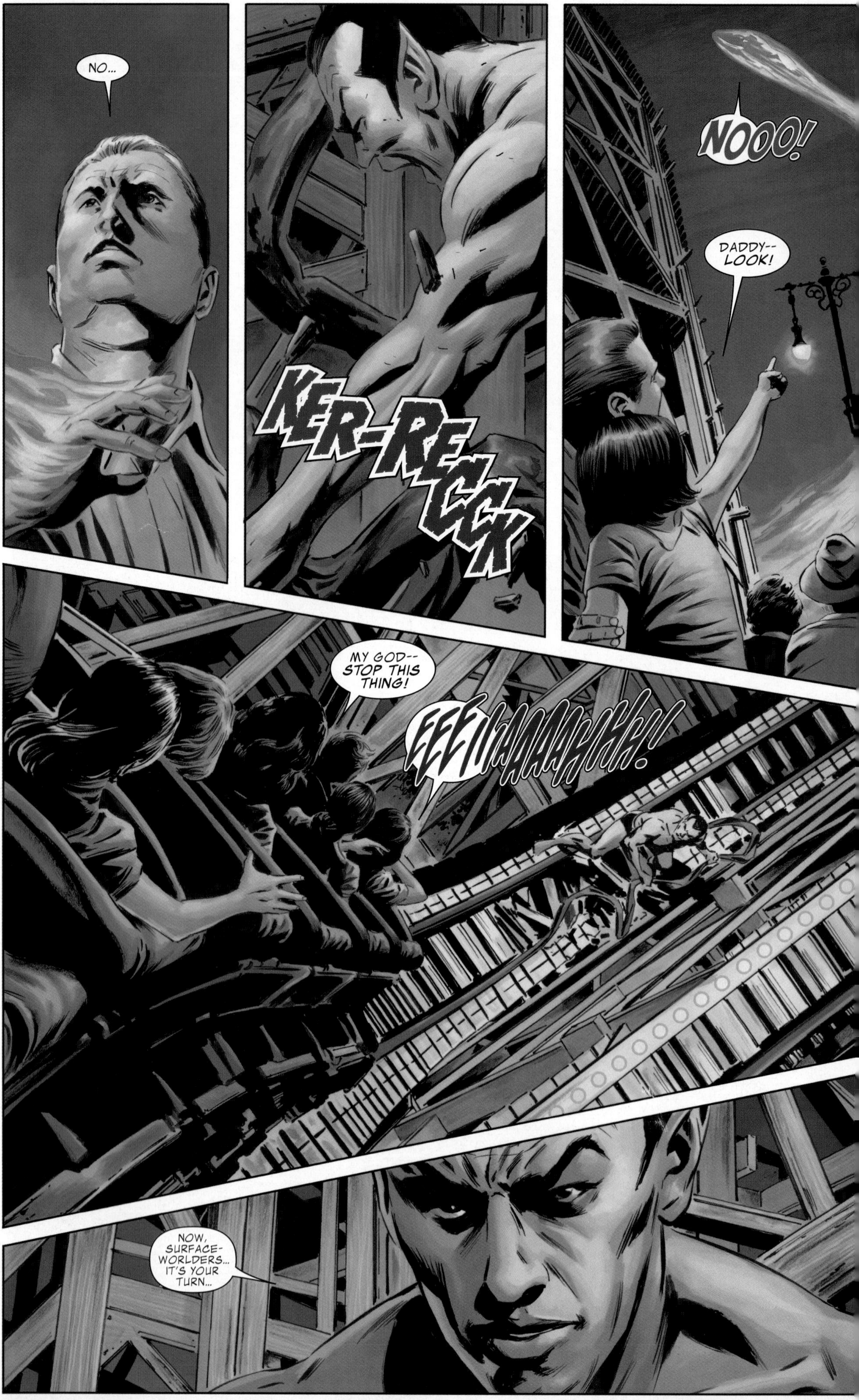
NO...
KER-RECCK
NOOO!
DADDY-- LOOK!
MY GOD-- STOP THIS THING!
EEEIIIAAAAAHHHH!
NOW, SURFACE-WORLDERS... IT'S YOUR TURN...

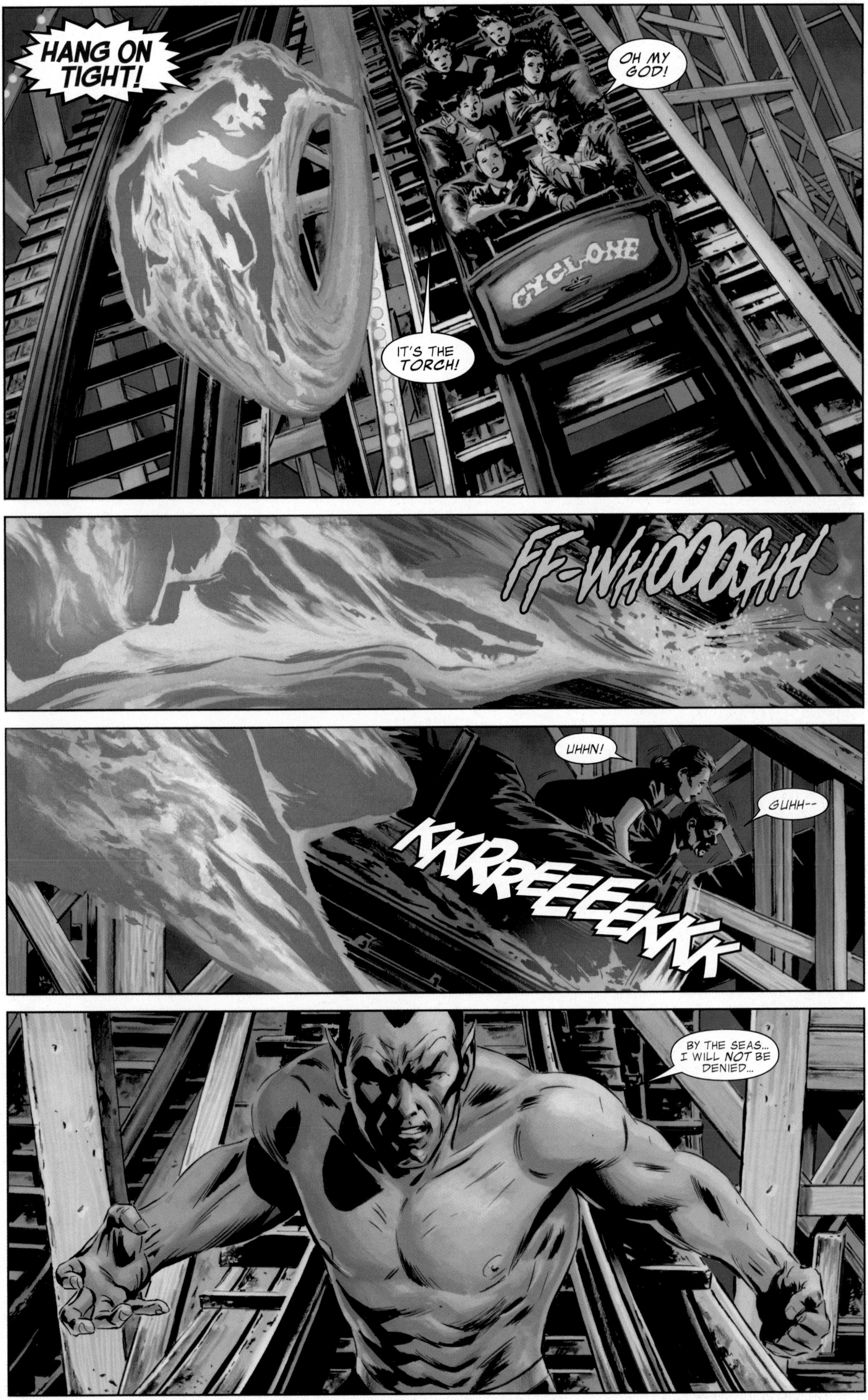
HANG ON TIGHT!
OH MY GOD!
IT'S THE TORCH!
CYCLONE
FF-WHOOOOSHH
UHHN!
GUHH--
KKRREEEEKKK
BY THE SEAS... I WILL NOT BE DENIED...

THIS DAY WOULD BE REMEMBERED FOR *MANY* REASONS.

IT WOULD BE THE FIRST TIME ANY HUMAN SAW NAMOR AND *LIVED* TO TELL ABOUT IT.

THE FIRST TIME WE KNEW *FOR SURE* A NEW AGE WAS UPON US...

...AN AGE OF *SUPERHUMANS*.

CYCLONE

BUT MOST OF NEW YORK WOULD REMEMBER THIS AS THE DAY THE HUMAN TORCH STOPPED BEING THOUGHT OF AS A MENACE...

...A MONSTER ON THE LOOSE...

...AND BECAME ONE OF OUR GREATEST HEROES.

FOR PRINCE NAMOR, OF COURSE...IT WOULD BE DIFFERENT.

FOR HIM THIS WAS A DAY OF GREAT SHAME AND DEFEAT.

ONE THAT WOULD BURN *FAR BEYOND* THE WOUNDS HE RECEIVED IN BATTLE.

THAT WOULD FOCUS HIS RAGE ON *NEW YORK*, ON THE PEOPLE WHO WOULD ONE DAY BE HIS ALLIES...

...AND NOT WHERE IT BELONGED.

BUT THE GREAT WAR WAITED OUT THERE FOR NAMOR, TOO, AS IT DID FOR ALL OF US...

SO, DO WE THINK HE WAS A *NAZI AGENT?*

DID YOU SEE THE PAPERS? LOOKED MORE ASIAN TO ME. MAYBE *JAPANESE...*

BUT WE HAVE *NO INTEL* ON HIM...

HE COULD BE A *ROGUE AGENT* FOR ALL WE KNOW.

GOD HELP US IF HE *IS,* KERMIT... THAT'S ALL WE NEED.

DON'T I KNOW IT...

SO, WHO ARE WE MEETING TODAY, GENERAL?

PROFESSOR ZOGOLOWSKI.

OH, RIGHT...THIS IS THE GIANT *ROBOT* THING... ELECTRO?

YEAH...OUR PEOPLE WENT OVER THE DESIGN SPECS AND THEY THINK IT'LL WORK.

REALLY? AND IT CAN DO 100 MILES AN HOUR?

WELL, LET'S SEE THE NAZIS TOP *THAT...*

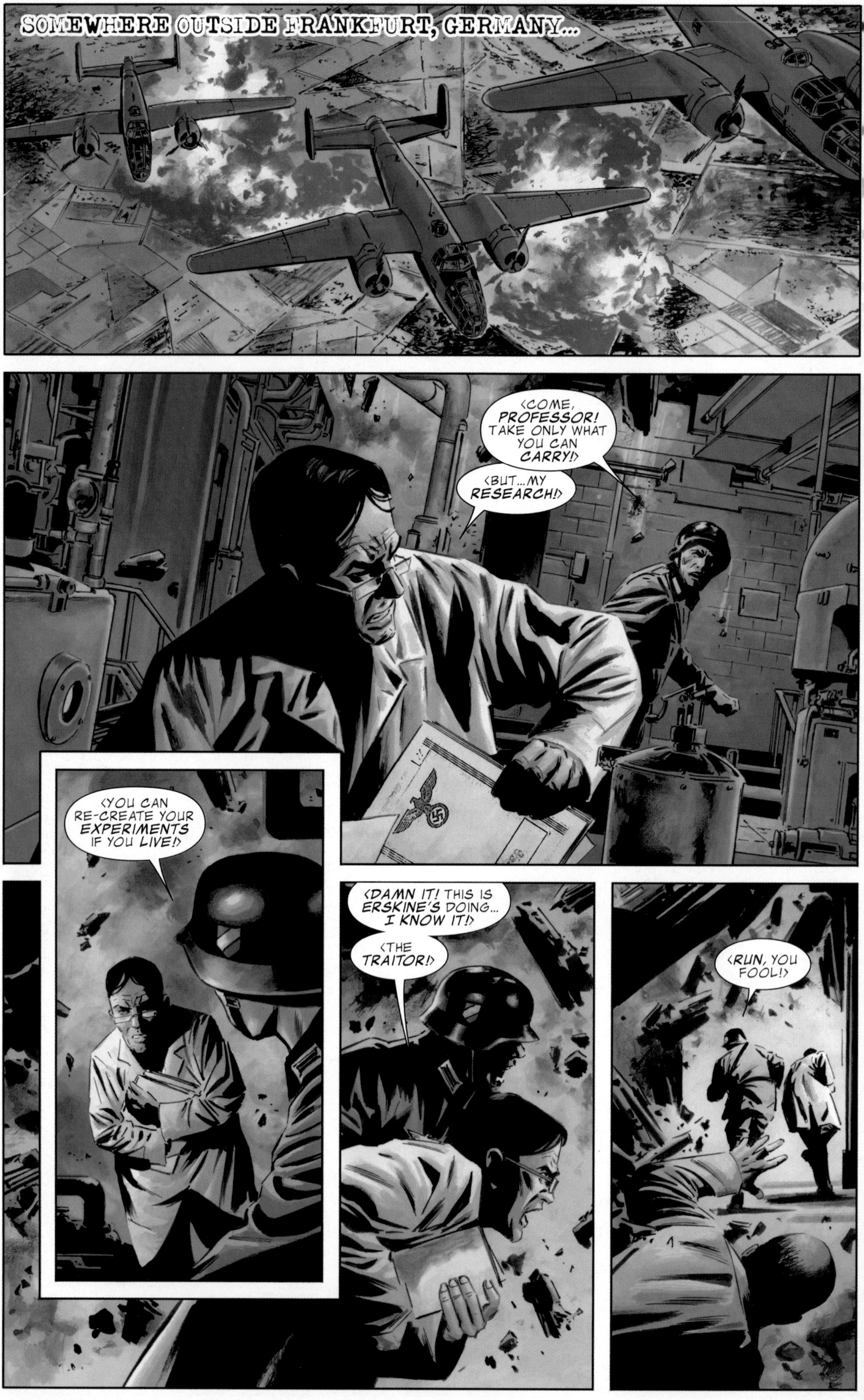
SOMEWHERE OUTSIDE FRANKFURT, GERMANY...
<COME, PROFESSOR! TAKE ONLY WHAT YOU CAN CARRY!>
<BUT...MY RESEARCH!>
<YOU CAN RE-CREATE YOUR EXPERIMENTS IF YOU LIVE!>
<DAMN IT! THIS IS ERSKINE'S DOING... I KNOW IT!>
<THE TRAITOR!>
<RUN, YOU FOOL!>

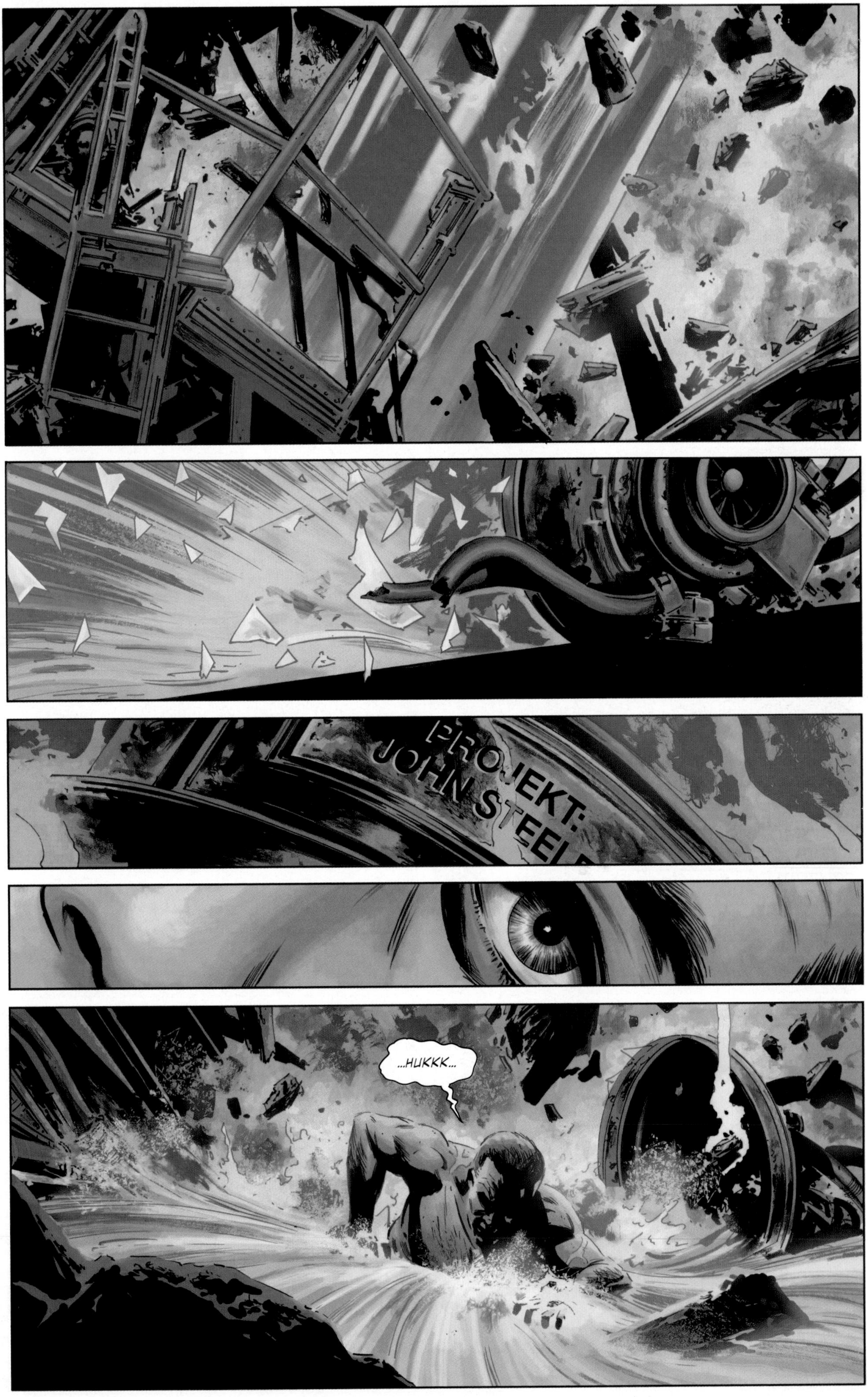
PROJEKT:
JOHN STEELE
...HUKKK...

ALTHOUGH NONE OF US KNEW IT AT THE TIME, THE ALLIES HAD JUST GIVEN THE NAZI SCIENCE EFFORT ITS *SECOND* MAJOR SETBACK.

AND *PRIVATE JOHN STEELE* HAD BEEN AWAKENED INTO A NEW WAR...

WHAT THE HELL...?

...OVER *TWENTY YEARS* SINCE HE'D BEEN CAPTURED DURING THE PREVIOUS ONE.

WHILE BACK HOME, THE NAZI SCIENCE EFFORT'S *FIRST* MAJOR SETBACK, PROFESSOR ERSKINE...

...WAS ABOUT TO CHANGE THE COURSE OF HISTORY.

The Marvels Project # 4 Cover by Steve Epting

The Marvels Project # 4 Variant Cover by Steve McNiven

PART FOUR

AS THE FALL BEGAN IN 1940, THERE WERE *SINISTER FORCES* MOVING IN THE SHADOWS OF NEW YORK CITY.

FOREIGN *AGENTS* MEETING IN THE NIGHT...

YOU'RE SURE YOU WERE NOT *FOLLOWED*, KRUGER?

NEIN, I--

SPEAK ENGLISH...

...OR DO YOU WISH TO BE *FOUND OUT* BEFORE YOUR MISSION EVEN *BEGINS*?

SORRY, MAJOR... IT WAS A *LONG* VOYAGE.

AND I DON'T ENJOY *U-BOATS* VERY MUCH.

BUT YOU GOT THROUGH WITH NO TROUBLE, YES?

WE HAD TO REMOVE AN INTERLOPER FROM THE DOCKS EARLIER THIS YEAR.

IT WAS A SMOOTH OPERATION ALL THE WAY, SIR.

GOOD, LET'S HOPE IT CONTINUES TO BE.

HAVE YOU GOT MY PAPERS?

WILL I HAVE ACCESS?

LIMITED ACCESS, BUT I HEARD YOU WERE BLESSED WITH MORE THAN A MODICUM OF INGENUITY.

YOUR NEW NAME IS FREDERICK CLEMSON...

AND YOU'RE SPECIAL AGENT FOR THE MINISTRY OF FOREIGN AFFAIRS.

AH, GOOD... YOU HAVE MY BACKGROUND?

IT'S ALL IN THE FILE.

AND *YOU?* YOU'VE GOTTEN INSIDE THE *TRAITOR'S* PROJECT?

YES. I'M WITHIN *DAYS* OF HAVING MY HANDS ON ERSKINE'S *FORMULA...*

AND ONCE I HAVE *THAT,* YOU'LL BE FREE TO ACT.

GOOD. THE SOONER THE BETTER.

HEINZ KRUGER HAD SPENT MONTHS TRAINING TO PASS AS AN AMERICAN.

CONSIDERED ONE OF THE NAZIS' *TOP* FIELD OPERATIVES...

...THIS WAS THE MAN HITLER HAD SENT TO *KILL* DR. ERSKINE AND STOP THE *SUPER-SOLDIER* PROJECT.

BUT WHILE KRUGER AND HIS CONTACT *MAJOR KERFOOT* WERE DANGEROUS MEN...

SEE, NOSIE... I *KNEW* THERE WAS SOMETHING FISHY ABOUT THIS *PROFESSOR HAMILTON.*

NOW YOU WAIT *HERE* WHILE I GO SEE WHERE THIS *FRIEND* OF HIS GOES...

...NEITHER WAS AS DEADLY AS THEIR *HANDLER.*

EXCUSE ME, SIR, COULD YOU HELP ME WITH SOMETHING?

SORRY, MAC, I'VE GOT PLACES TO BE...

I'M AFRAID YOU'RE MISTAKEN...

HEY--?

AHH!

...GUHH...

MY GOD... WHAT ARE YOU *DOING*?

THIS ONE WAS *FOLLOWING* YOU.

HE *CAN'T* HAVE BEEN... WHO IS HE?

FERRET INVESTIGATIONS.

THE FERRET CONFIDENTIAL INVESTIGATIONS

HE'S A *PRIVATE EYE*?

GET TO THE *SAFE HOUSE*... I'LL SEARCH HIS OFFICE AND FIND OUT WHAT HE *KNOWS*.

WE'RE *TOO CLOSE* NOW FOR ANY MISTAKES...

KRUGER'S MISSION FOR HITLER WAS EVEN MORE *URGENT* THAN HE'D REALIZED WHEN HE LEFT HIS HOMELAND.

ACCORDING TO MAJOR KERFOOT'S REPORT...

...DAMN...

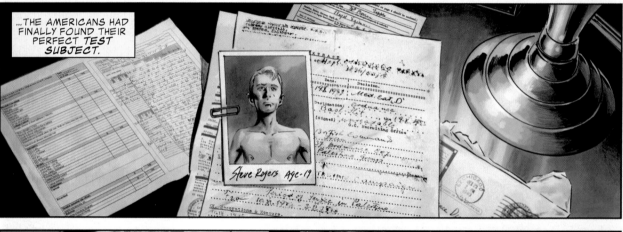

...THE AMERICANS HAD FINALLY FOUND THEIR PERFECT *TEST SUBJECT.*

Steve Rogers Age-19

KERFOOT HAD EVEN MANAGED TO *COPY* THE ENTIRE DOSSIER ON *STEVE ROGERS.*

TEST SUBJECT: **PROJECT REBIRTH**
BACKGROUND

A NATIVE NEW YORKER WHO'D COME OF AGE AT THE HEIGHT OF THE *GREAT DEPRESSION...*

HIS FATHER HAD DIED WHILE HE WAS JUST A BOY, AND HIS MOTHER HAD STRUGGLED TO RAISE HIM...

BUT STEVE WAS A *SICKLY* CHILD.

A *SKINNY* YOUTH WHO WAS A FREQUENT TARGET FOR *BULLIES* WHILE GROWING UP.

GET THE *STRING-BEAN!* GET 'IM!

AND AN *ARTISTIC* TYPE, WHO HAD STUDIED AS A PAINTER AND ILLUSTRATOR.

HIS MOTHER'S DEATH FROM *PNEUMONIA* THREE YEARS EARLIER HAD LEFT HIM VIRTUALLY ALONE...

I'M SORRY, SON...

...TO FEND *FOR HIMSELF* AT AGE 16, ON THE HARSH STREETS OF NEW YORK IN THE 1930s.

AND IF NOT FOR THE *NAZI INVASION* OF POLAND, PERHAPS STEVE ROGERS *WOULD* HAVE BECOME A PAINTER, INSTEAD OF A *TEST SUBJECT.*

BUT IT TURNED OUT THAT ROGERS, FOR ALL HIS FRAILTY, WAS *NOT A COWARD.*

AFTER SEEING NEWSREELS OF *HITLER'S SOLDIERS* MARCHING ACROSS EUROPE...

...ROGERS TRIED *SEVERAL TIMES* TO ENLIST IN THE ARMY.

KID, C'MON... WHY'RE YOU *WASTING MY TIME?*

JUST PUT ME ON THE *SCALE...* I *KNOW* I'VE PUT ON WEIGHT...

BUT EACH TIME HE WAS *TURNED AWAY.*

SORRY, KIDDO... I'M AFRAID UNCLE SAM CAN'T TAKE YOU...

YOU'RE A 4-F.

BUT ROGERS' *DETERMINATION* ATTRACTED THE ATTENTION OF *GENERAL PHILLIPS,* WHO WAS OVERSEEING ERSKINE'S EXPERIMENT.

DOC... LET ME SEE THAT LAST ONE'S *PAPERWORK...*

AND AFTER A THOROUGH BACKGROUND CHECK, THE GENERAL APPROACHED HIM.

IF YOU *REALLY* WANT TO SERVE YOUR COUNTRY, I'VE GOT AN *OFFER* FOR YOU...

WHAT'S THE *CATCH,* GENERAL?

THE CATCH IS THERE'S A *GOOD CHANCE* YOU WON'T *SURVIVE...*

...BUT NONE OF US *LIVE FOREVER,* DO WE?

AND SO, FOR TWO MONTHS, STEVE ROGERS HAD BEEN UNDERGOING *EXTENSIVE TESTING* UNDER PROFESSOR ERSKINE'S SUPERVISION.

ALL IN PREPARATION FOR AN *EXPERIMENTAL PROCEDURE* THAT MIGHT KILL HIM.

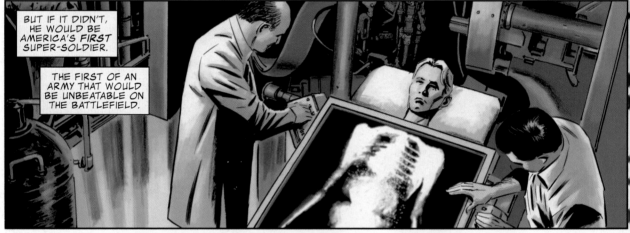

BUT IF IT DIDN'T, HE WOULD BE AMERICA'S *FIRST* SUPER-SOLDIER.

THE FIRST OF AN ARMY THAT WOULD BE UNBEATABLE ON THE BATTLEFIELD.

IN HIS SAFE-HOUSE, HEINZ KRUGER FELT THE WEIGHT OF HIS MISSION, FINALLY, AND KNEW THAT FAILURE WAS NOT AN OPTION.

BECAUSE *FEW THINGS* WERE MORE TROUBLING THAN A MAN LIKE STEVE ROGERS...

...WHO HAD NO FEAR OF *DEATH.*

BUT I KNEW NOTHING OF THIS THEN...

I WOULD ONLY FIND OUT *MUCH LATER* WHAT HAPPENED IN MY CITY THAT NIGHT.

NO...

I HAD CROSSED PATHS WITH *THE FERRET* A FEW TIMES. HE WAS A GOOD MAN.

ANOTHER GOOD MAN LEFT TO *DIE* IN AN ALLEY.

DAMN IT...

HELLO THERE...I THINK YOU'RE CALLED *NOSIE*, RIGHT?

YOU'D BETTER COME WITH ME.

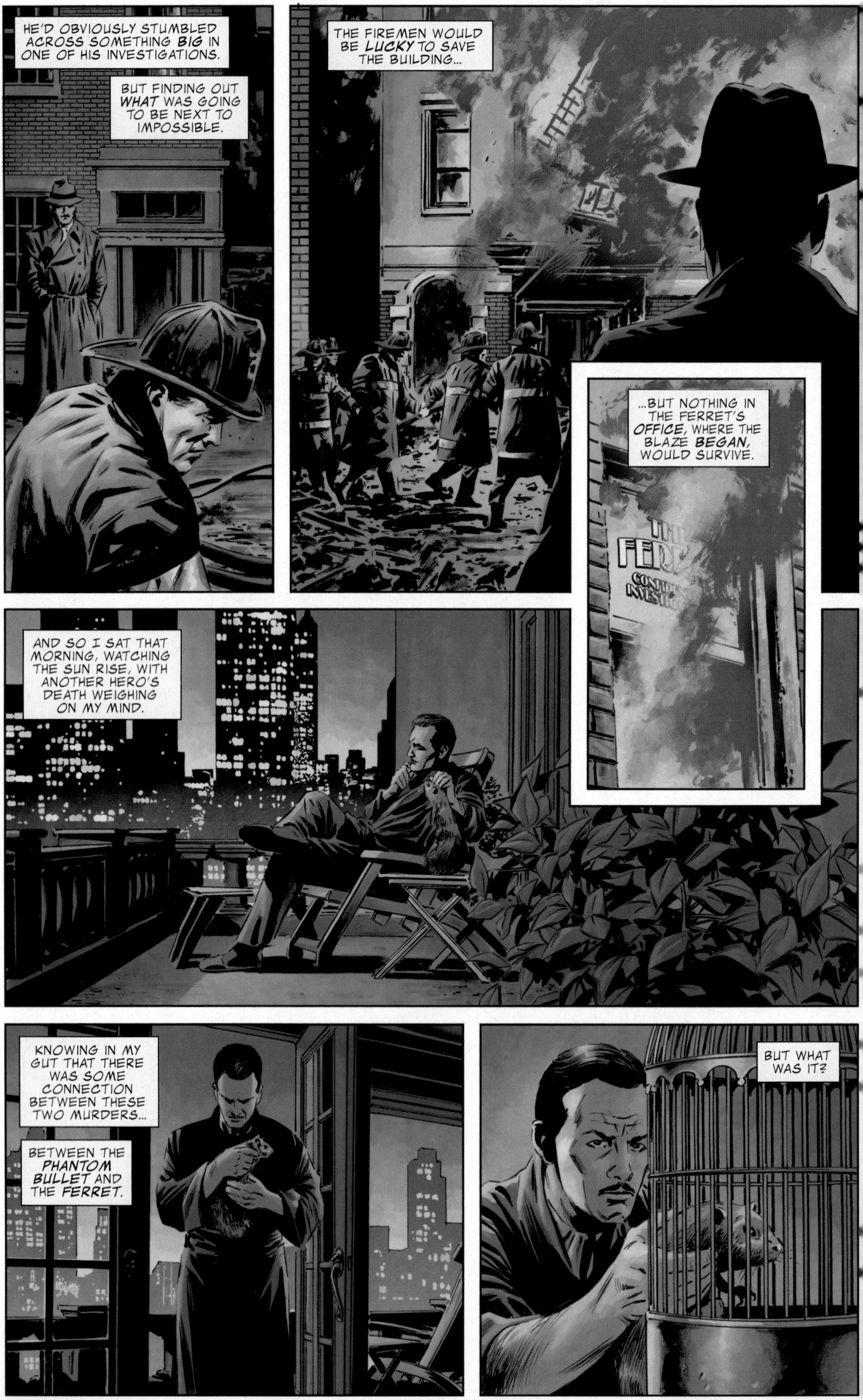
HE'D OBVIOUSLY STUMBLED ACROSS SOMETHING BIG IN ONE OF HIS INVESTIGATIONS.
BUT FINDING OUT WHAT WAS GOING TO BE NEXT TO IMPOSSIBLE.
THE FIREMEN WOULD BE LUCKY TO SAVE THE BUILDING...
...BUT NOTHING IN THE FERRET'S OFFICE, WHERE THE BLAZE BEGAN, WOULD SURVIVE.
AND SO I SAT THAT MORNING, WATCHING THE SUN RISE, WITH ANOTHER HERO'S DEATH WEIGHING ON MY MIND.
KNOWING IN MY GUT THAT THERE WAS SOME CONNECTION BETWEEN THESE TWO MURDERS...
BETWEEN THE PHANTOM BULLET AND THE FERRET.
BUT WHAT WAS IT?

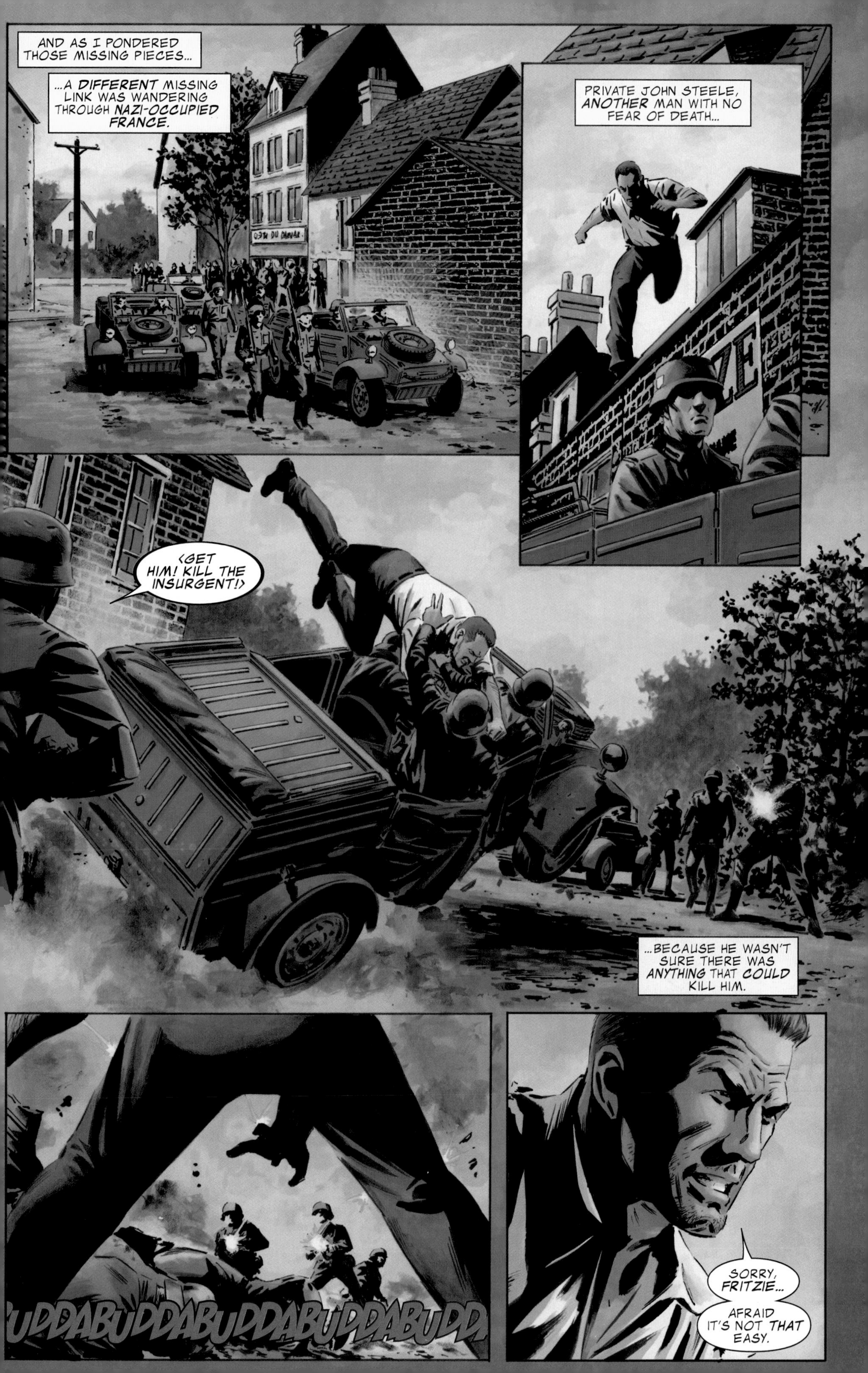
AND AS I PONDERED THOSE MISSING PIECES...
...A DIFFERENT MISSING LINK WAS WANDERING THROUGH NAZI-OCCUPIED FRANCE.
PRIVATE JOHN STEELE, ANOTHER MAN WITH NO FEAR OF DEATH...
<GET HIM! KILL THE INSURGENT!>
...BECAUSE HE WASN'T SURE THERE WAS ANYTHING THAT COULD KILL HIM.
BUDDABUDDABUDDABUDDABUDD
SORRY, FRITZIE...
AFRAID IT'S NOT THAT EASY.

STEELE HAD SPENT THE LAST FEW MONTHS *REACQUAINTING* HIMSELF WITH THE WORLD.

ALTHOUGH *TECHNOLOGY* HAD IMPROVED, HE FOUND *THE PEOPLE* WERE MUCH THE SAME.

THE SAME HATREDS, SAME FEARS, SAME WARS...

HE COULD NO LONGER REMEMBER HOW MANY BATTLES HE'D BEEN IN...

...BUT FIGHTING THE *GERMANS* FELT LIKE THE RIGHT THING TO DO.

WHAT IN HELL ARE YOU *DOING*, KRUGER?

IT'S OVER A *WEEK* SINCE YOU GAINED ACCESS, AND YET PROFESSOR ERSKINE IS STILL *BREATHING*, IS HE NOT?

IT'S NOT AS *EASY* AS YOU THINK...

"...FOR ONE, HE'S SELDOM *ALONE*.

HAND ME THAT BEAKER, WOULD YOU, MY DEAR?

"HE'S WITH HIS ASSISTANTS, OTHER SCIENTISTS, OR *MILITARY PERSONNEL* AT NEARLY *ALL* TIMES."

AND WHAT'S OUR *TIMETABLE* LOOKING LIKE?

ONE *CANNOT* RUSH GENIUS, GENERAL PHILLIPS.

AND ONE CAN'T SAY *THAT* TO THE *PRESIDENT*, PROFESSOR...

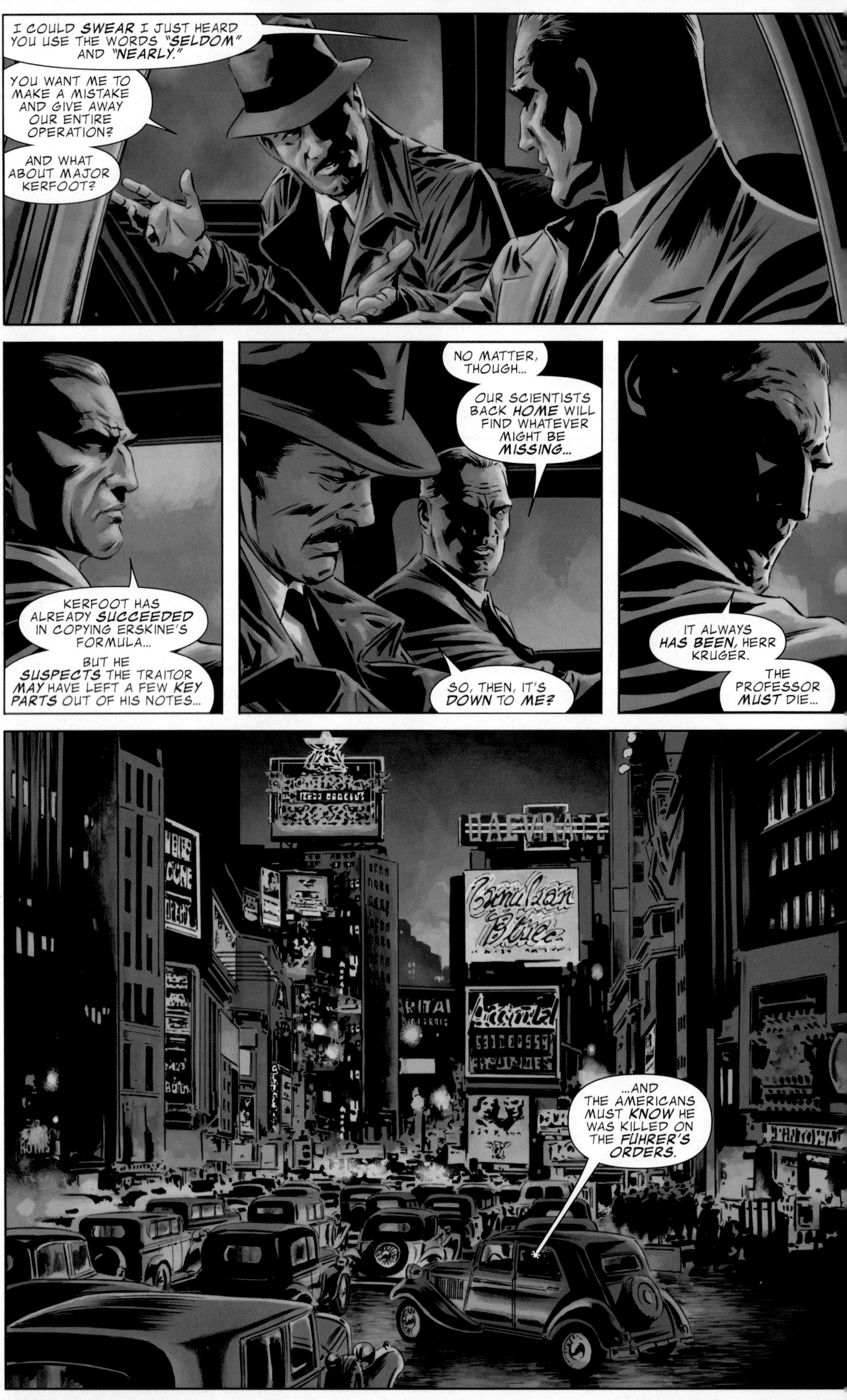
I COULD SWEAR I JUST HEARD YOU USE THE WORDS "SELDOM" AND "NEARLY."
YOU WANT ME TO MAKE A MISTAKE AND GIVE AWAY OUR ENTIRE OPERATION?
AND WHAT ABOUT MAJOR KERFOOT?
KERFOOT HAS ALREADY SUCCEEDED IN COPYING ERSKINE'S FORMULA...
BUT HE SUSPECTS THE TRAITOR MAY HAVE LEFT A FEW KEY PARTS OUT OF HIS NOTES...
NO MATTER, THOUGH...
OUR SCIENTISTS BACK HOME WILL FIND WHATEVER MIGHT BE MISSING...
SO, THEN, IT'S DOWN TO ME?
IT ALWAYS HAS BEEN, HERR KRUGER.
THE PROFESSOR MUST DIE...
...AND THE AMERICANS MUST KNOW HE WAS KILLED ON THE FÜHRER'S ORDERS.

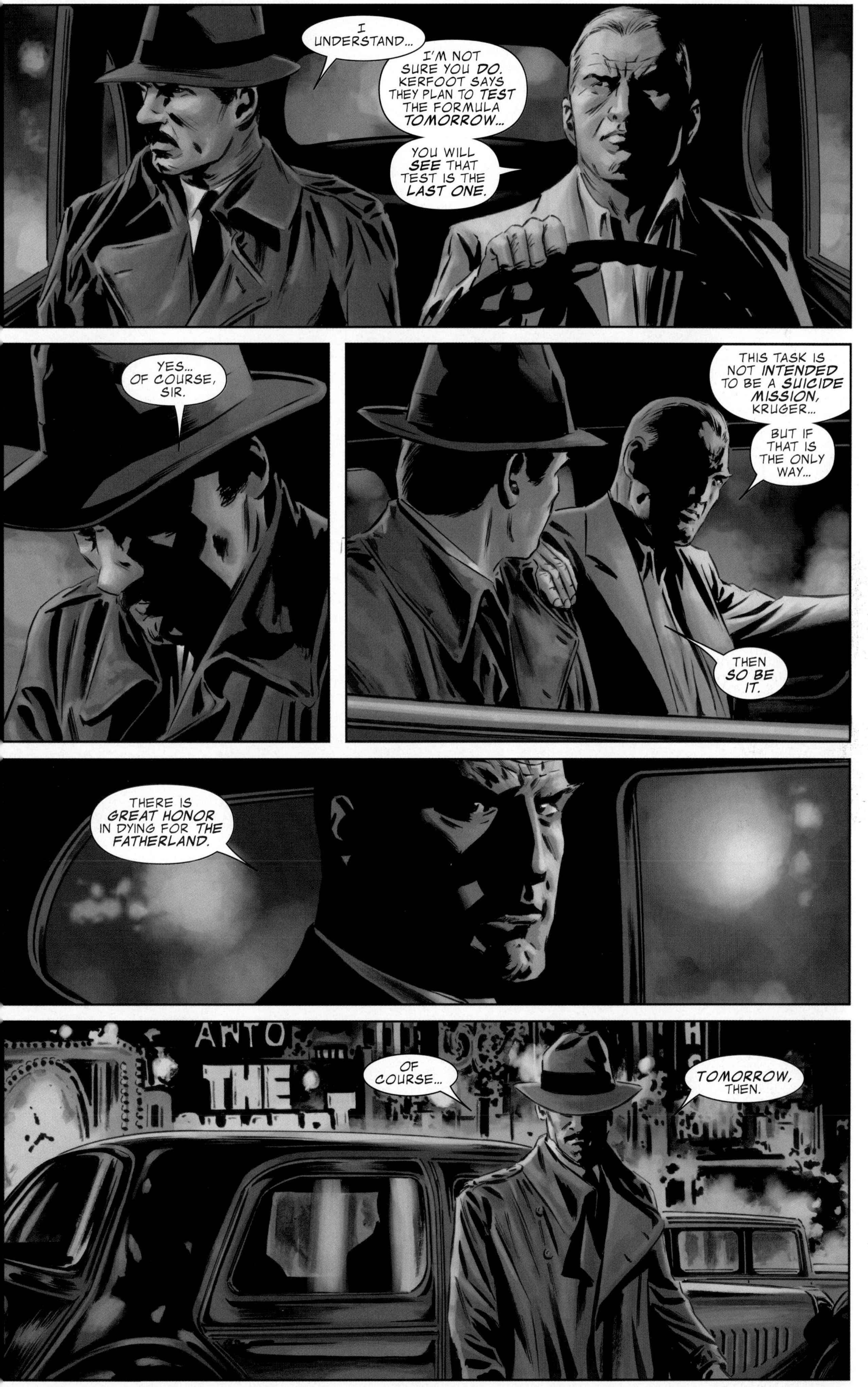
I UNDERSTAND...
I'M NOT SURE YOU DO. KERFOOT SAYS THEY PLAN TO TEST THE FORMULA TOMORROW...
YOU WILL SEE THAT TEST IS THE LAST ONE.
YES... OF COURSE, SIR.
THIS TASK IS NOT INTENDED TO BE A SUICIDE MISSION, KRUGER...
BUT IF THAT IS THE ONLY WAY...
THEN SO BE IT.
THERE IS GREAT HONOR IN DYING FOR THE FATHERLAND.
OF COURSE...
TOMORROW, THEN.

THAT NIGHT, IN HIS SAFE HOUSE, HEINZ KRUGER WROTE A *LETTER* TO HIS WIFE THAT WOULD *NEVER* BE MAILED...

My dearest Elise, If you do not hear from me again, tell our children their father died a hero...

...in this foreign land, where these wide-eyed Americans see only their bright lights.

They know nothing of the real world, or of the suffering in Europe, they know nothing of history.

How I hate them, and how I wish I was on German soil once again, and in your arms.

But for the glory of the Eternal Reich, I must say goodbye to all I love.

Remember me as your faithful husband, Heinz

SPECIAL AGENT CLEMSON... FOREIGN AFFAIRS MINISTRY...

YES, SIR...

IF THEY ONLY KNEW WHAT WE WERE *DOING* DOWN HERE BELOW GROUND...

IT'S TRULY A *WONDER* TO BEHOLD, ISN'T IT?

YES...
YES, IT TRULY
IS...

NEVER
THOUGHT I'D
LIVE TO SEE
ANYTHING LIKE
THIS.

YOU AND
ME *BOTH,*
FELLA.

BUT THIS
IS *IT...*THE
BIG DAY...

THE *GAME*
CHANGER...

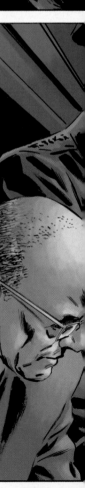

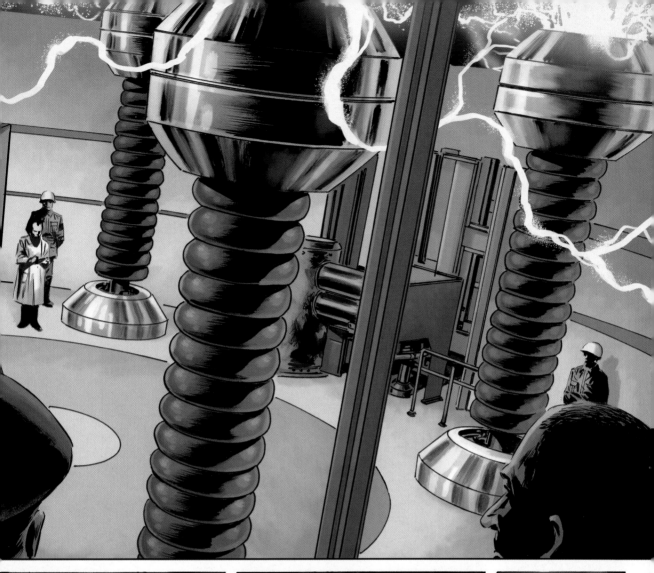

AFTER TODAY, HITLER WON'T STAND A CHANCE WHEN WE GET INTO THIS WAR.

YES...

THIS *IS* THE BIG DAY...

The Marvels Project # 5 Cover by Steve Epting

PART FIVE

STEVE ROGERS' LIFE DIDN'T GET ANY EASIER AFTER HIS *TRANSFORMATION.*

HIS *NEW BROAD SHOULDERS* WERE INSTANTLY WEIGHED DOWN BY AN *INCREDIBLE* BURDEN.

ONE HE COULDN'T STOP *THINKING* ABOUT, NO MATTER HOW HARD HE TRAINED...

THE DAY OF THE *EXPERIMENT*--HIS *REBIRTH*--WAS MEANT TO BE A DAY OF *HOPE.*

A DAY OF AMERICAN TRIUMPH.

AND IT *WAS.*

PROFESSOR ERSKINE'S *SUPER-SOLDIER SERUM* HAD WORKED.

BUT THERE WAS *NO* CELEBRATION.

JUST SHOTS RINGING OUT...

BLAM BLAM BLAM

...AND *BETRAYAL.*

LONG LIVE THE THIRD REICH!

STEVE'S FIRST MOMENTS AS AMERICA'S SUPER-SOLDIER, THEN...

...ONLY ADDED TO THE TRAGEDY.

HE'D ACTED IN HASTE, NOT UNDERSTANDING HIS NEW STRENGTH.

IT WAS TOO LATE WHEN HE REALIZED THE NAZI SPY WAS DEAD.

AND IT WAS TOO LATE FOR PROFESSOR ERSKINE... AND THE ENTIRE SUPER-SOLDIER PROGRAM.

BECAUSE ERSKINE HAD NEVER WRITTEN DOWN HIS ENTIRE FORMULA.

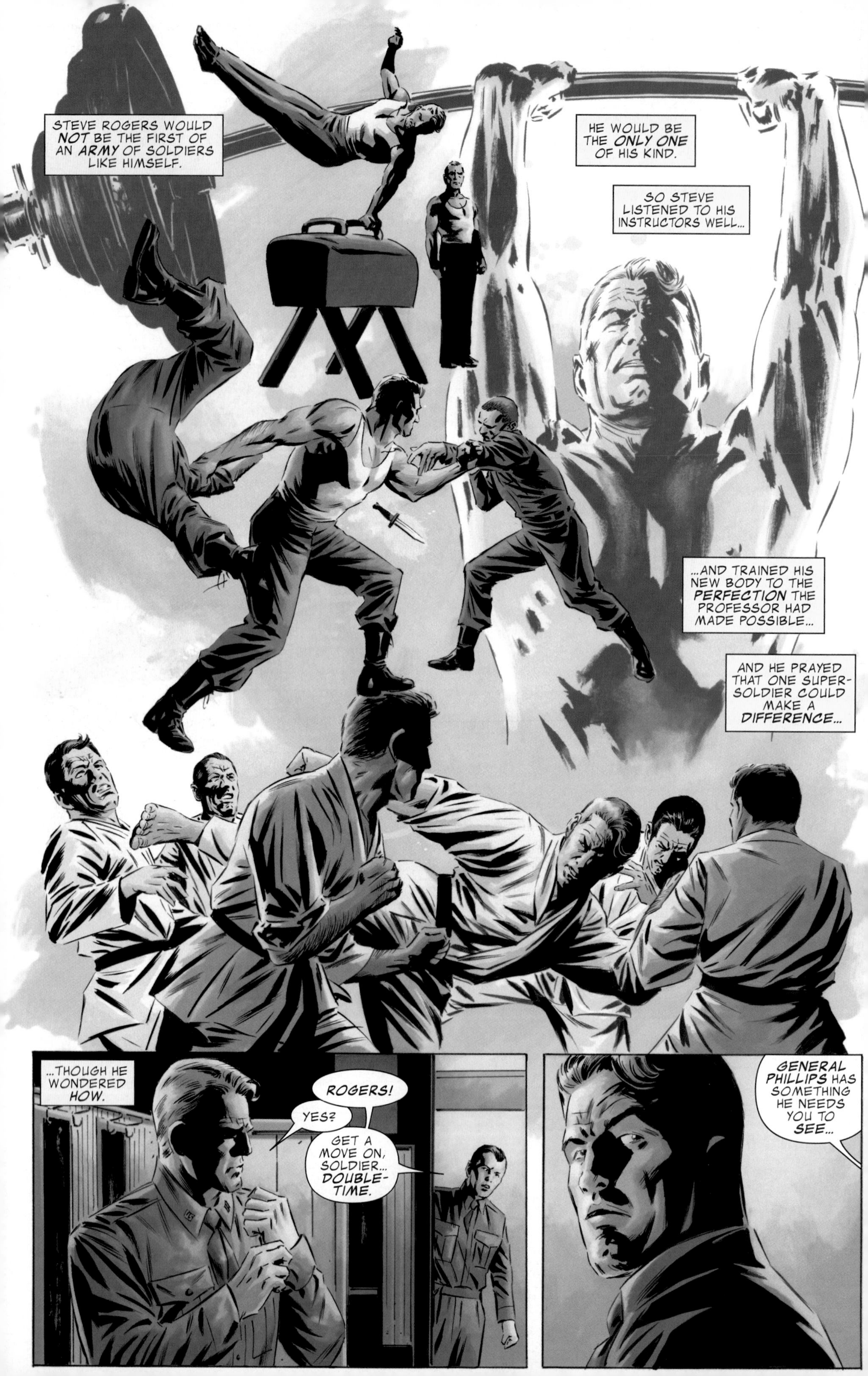
STEVE ROGERS WOULD NOT BE THE FIRST OF AN ARMY OF SOLDIERS LIKE HIMSELF.
HE WOULD BE THE ONLY ONE OF HIS KIND.
SO STEVE LISTENED TO HIS INSTRUCTORS WELL...
...AND TRAINED HIS NEW BODY TO THE PERFECTION THE PROFESSOR HAD MADE POSSIBLE...
AND HE PRAYED THAT ONE SUPER-SOLDIER COULD MAKE A DIFFERENCE...
...THOUGH HE WONDERED HOW.
ROGERS!
YES?
GET A MOVE ON, SOLDIER... DOUBLE-TIME.
GENERAL PHILLIPS HAS SOMETHING HE NEEDS YOU TO SEE...

NEW YORK CITY.

BUT THE DAYS AFTER ERSKINE'S *ASSASSINATION* HADN'T GONE WELL FOR NAZI SPY *MAJOR KERFOOT,* EITHER.

HE'D FLED HIS APARTMENT, ONLY HOURS BEFORE *GOVERNMENT AGENTS* HAD KICKED DOWN THE DOOR.

AND THE NEXT MORNING, HE FAKED HIS OWN DEATH IN A *CAR BOMB.*

BUT HE STILL SAW EYES WATCHING HIM AROUND EVERY CORNER.

HE STILL COULDN'T *SLEEP.*

NO, HE WOULDN'T SLEEP UNTIL HE WAS SAFELY BACK HOME IN GERMANY.

KNOK KNOK

LET ME *IN.*

WHO'S THIS WITH YOU?

FRIENDS. WHO DO YOU THINK?

HAS--HAS THE *FORMULA* BEEN RECEIVED BACK IN BERLIN?

YES... THEY'RE ALREADY *AT WORK* ON IT.

YOU MADE NO *OTHER* COPIES, CORRECT?

I DON'T...I'M NOT *SURE*...

I MAY HAVE WRITTEN *PART* OF IT IN ONE OF MY NOTEBOOKS...

YOU'RE *NOT SURE?*

I HAVEN'T-- HAVEN'T BEEN *SLEEPING.*

AND IT WAS A LONG MISSION...CAN'T RECALL *EVERY* DETAIL OF IT...

SO I *SEE*...

WHEN DO I GET TO GO *HOME?*

TODAY, ALBRECHT...

WHUU--

...YOU GO HOME TODAY.

KRIK

ALL RIGHT... CLEAN THIS MESS UP...

GET RID OF HIS BODY SO IT'S NEVER FOUND. UNDERSTAND?

YES, SIR.

AND PACK UP HIS BOOKS.

THEY'LL NEED TO BE SHIPPED BACK TO GERMANY.

GEHEIM-AKTE VON SS MAJ. KERFOOT

A WEEK EARLIER, I'D FOUND THE FERRET'S *LAST CLIENT*, A WOMAN WHOSE MOTHER HAD *GONE MISSING*.

FOLLOWING THE SAME CLUES HE HAD LED TO THE MAN I'D COME TO KNOW AS *MAJOR KERFOOT*.

BUT HIS BUILDING WAS UNDER *GOVERNMENT GUARD*.

THEN THE PIECES FELL INTO PLACE.

THE FERRET HAD STUMBLED ACROSS A *NAZI SPY*, AND IT HAD GOTTEN HIM KILLED.

SO I WORKED *THAT* ANGLE.

I'M LOOKING FOR MEN WITH *GERMAN ACCENTS* HIDING IN THE CITY!

SOMEONE *HAS* TO KNOW WHERE THEY ARE!

TALK!

BUT THE STREETS WEREN'T TALKING, SO I HAD TO TRY SOMETHING ELSE.

THE PEN *and* THE SWORD

YOU'RE KELLERMAN? FROM THE *BUGLE?*

Y-YEAH...?

YOU WROTE ABOUT THE SCIENTIST WHO DIED A FEW WEEKS AGO.

SURE...SURE... OKAY.

WHAT'VE YOU HEARD ABOUT *NAZI SPIES* IN THE CITY?

NOTHING I CAN PRINT... BUT WE *KNOW* THEY'RE HERE...

THAT *PROFESSOR* WHO GOT KILLED? IT WAS *NAZIS* WHO DID THAT.

WHY?

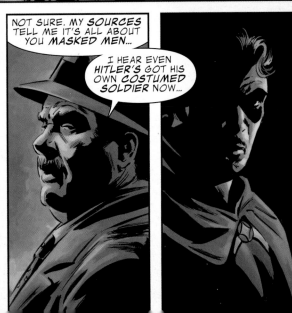

NOT SURE. MY *SOURCES* TELL ME IT'S ALL ABOUT YOU *MASKED MEN...*

I HEAR EVEN *HITLER'S* GOT HIS OWN *COSTUMED SOLDIER* NOW...

"...IF YOU CAN BELIEVE THAT."

<NO! PLEASE!>

<WE'RE NOT RESISTANCE! PLEASE! I BEG YOU!>

<DON'T BE RIDICULOUS, WOMAN...>

<...I DON'T CARE IF YOU AND YOUR HUSBAND ARE PART OF THEIR PLOT.>

<I DON'T CARE IF HALF THIS TOWN IS INNOCENT...>

<THE RED SKULL IS HERE TO MAKE A POINT.>

BUDDABUDDABUDDABUDDABUDDA

<NOW THEN...I WANT TO KNOW WHERE THE *AMERICAN* AND THE *BRITISH* FIGHTERS ARE.>

<SOMEONE HAS BEEN *HIDING THEM* IN YOUR VILLAGES...>

<SOMEONE KNOWS WHERE THEY ARE RIGHT NOW.>

<ALL IT TAKES IS *ONE* OF YOU...TO END THIS.>

<PLEASE... PLEASE...NO...>

<WE DO NOT *KNOW* THESE MEN...>

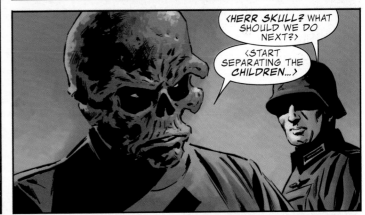

<*HERR SKULL?* WHAT SHOULD WE DO NEXT?>

<START SEPARATING THE *CHILDREN*...>

<...AND *LINE THEM UP* ALONG THE WALL.>

...THEY'RE ALL DEAD...

...EVEN THE WOMEN AND CHILDREN...

THOSE NAZI BASTARDS.

OUR SCOUT SAYS SOME ESCAPED TO THE FOREST...BUT I HEAR YA, STEELE.

DO WE KNOW WHERE HE IS? THAT SKULL-MASKED CREEP?

I'M GOING TO KILL HIM WITH MY OWN HANDS.

NAH, OUR INTEL ON HITLER'S FREAK IS SHAKY AT BEST.

ANYWAY, I BEEN MEANIN' TO TELL YA', ME AN' RED ARE HEADIN' HOME...

...BACK TO THE STATES.

WHAT? WHY? THE WAR IS OVER HERE, FURY.

I KNOW, BUT THE *SKY DEVILS* HAVE BEEN ORDERED BACK TO OL' BLIGHTY...

AN' LIEUTENANT SAWYER REQUESTED OUR PRESENCE *STATESIDE.*

IT'S BECAUSE WE'VE STIRRED UP TOO MUCH *TROUBLE* HERE, ISN'T IT?

I'M NOT SURE *WHAT* THEY WANT... MILITARY AIN'T *BIG* ON EXPLANATIONS...

...BUT I WANNA KNOW IF YOU'RE COMIN' *WITH* US.

I KNOW THEY'D LOVE TO MEET YA... GUY WITH YOUR *ABILITIES.*

NO. MY PLACE IS *HERE,* NICK...

THESE PEOPLE DIED BECAUSE OF *US.* I WON'T SEE THAT GO UNPUNISHED...

AND BESIDES...FIRST THING THEY'D DO WITH ME *BACK HOME* IS START POKING AND PRODDING...

TRYING TO FIND OUT *HOW* I AM WHAT I AM...

"...AND I'M *THROUGH* BEING A SCIENCE PROJECT."

‹AH, PROFESSOR BRUDER... I WAS JUST GOING OVER YOUR NOTATIONS ON THE *JOHN STEELE EXPERIMENT...*›

‹DID ANY *TISSUE SAMPLES* SURVIVE THE EVACUATION OF YOUR PREVIOUS FACILITY?›

‹I'M AFRAID NOT, *BURSTEIN...* I KNOW YOU AREN'T USED TO *AIR RAIDS* IN SWITZERLAND...›

‹...BUT THEY *AREN'T* KIND TO SCIENTIFIC DATA.›

‹NO, I DON'T SUPPOSE THEY *WOULD* BE...›

‹SHAME.›

‹SO...HOW ARE YOU *SETTLING IN?* IT'S JUST YOU AND YOUR *SON?*›

‹YES, NOAH...WHO WOULD LOVE TO MEET YOU, I'M SURE...›

‹HE'S BEEN BOTHERING ME ABOUT MY WORK SINCE THE DAY WE ARRIVED.›

‹INTERESTED IN SCIENCE, IS HE?›

‹YES, LIKE FATHER LIKE SON, AS THEY SAY.›

‹WELL, YOU'D DO BEST TO KEEP HIM AWAY FROM HERE... THERE ARE THINGS IN THIS PLACE NO CHILD SHOULD SEE.›

‹YES... AGREED.›

‹AND HOW GOES YOUR NEW TASK? ANY PROGRESS MADE ON ERSKINE'S PARTIAL FORMULA?›

‹NO. NO GOOD NEWS THERE...HANLON THINKS WE MAY BE CLOSE TO CRACKING IT....›

‹...BUT WE DON'T EVEN KNOW IF ERSKINE'S TEST WAS A SUCCESS....›

BUT BACK IN NEW YORK, STEVE ROGERS WAS UNDERGOING A *SECOND* REBIRTH... IN A MANNER OF SPEAKING.

AS HE PUT ON THE UNIFORM PRESIDENT ROOSEVELT HAD *ASSIGNED* TO HIM...

...HE KEPT THINKING OF THE FILM HE'D WATCHED WITH GENERAL PHILLIPS.

THE *RED SKULL* ON HIS MARCH OF TERROR... HITLER'S *NEW* RIGHT HAND.

MASKS, SYMBOLS...THEY WERE TAKING ON A *LARGER LIFE* IN THESE TROUBLED TIMES.

HE THOUGHT ABOUT THE RECENT PHOTOS IN THE PRESS OF THE CRIME-FIGHTING *THIN MAN,* OR *HURRICANE,* WHO WAS SAID TO RUN AT SUPERHUMAN SPEED...

AND HE WONDERED IF HE WAS JOINING THEIR RANKS, OR IF HE WAS STILL A *SOLDIER*.

BUT MOSTLY HE THOUGHT ABOUT THE NAZI SPIES HE WAS BEING SENT AFTER THAT NIGHT.

IT HAD TAKEN ME *DAYS* TO TRACK THESE SAME SPIES AND I FOUND MYSELF BACK AT THE *WHARF...* WHERE MY QUEST HAD BEGUN SO LONG AGO.

AS IT TURNED OUT, I WAS JUST IN TIME TO WITNESS THE FIRST APPEARANCE...

...OF A TRUE MARVEL.

NEIN!

SKKKASSH

I'D NEVER SEEN *ANYONE* MOVE THE WAY HE DID--SO QUICK, SO EFFICIENT.

I WAS GOOD...

...BUT THIS MAN WAS SOMETHING ELSE *ENTIRELY*.

OF COURSE, IT DIDN'T SEEM LIKE HE *NEEDED* ANY HELP...

...UNTIL I NOTICED THE ONE THAT LOOKED LIKE THE *LEADER* TAKING IT ON THE LAM.

I'D COME FOR ANSWERS, AND *THIS* WAS THE MAN WHO WOULD HAVE THEM.

BUT I WAS A STEP OR TWO BEHIND, STILL THINKING ABOUT THE OTHER MAN, THE ONE IN THE BLUE AND RED SUIT...

...AND IT NEARLY GOT ME *KILLED*.

BUDDA BUDDA BUDDA BUDDA BUDDA

BUT JUST NEARLY.

AHH!

BUDDA BUDDA BUDDA BUDDA

STAY DOWN!

KEEP PRESSURE ON THIS. I'LL HAVE AN AMBULANCE HERE SOON.

IT'S OKAY, I'M A DOCTOR... JUST A FLESH WOUND.

HURTS LIKE HELL, THOUGH.

YOU'RE THE ANGEL, RIGHT? I READ ABOUT YOU.

WHAT ARE YOU DOING HERE?

INVESTIGATING THE *MURDERS* OF A FEW *OTHER* HEROES...

SEEMS THEY *CROSSED PATHS* WITH THE SAME NAZI SPIES *YOU* WERE HUNTING.

SORRY I GOT IN YOUR WAY.

NO... I'M *GLAD* TO MEET YOU.

BUT I'VE GOT MORE WORK TO DO...SURE YOU'LL BE OKAY?

LIKE I SAID, I'M A *DOCTOR*...WHEN I'M *NOT* WEARING A MASK.

THEN I'M OFF.

WAIT... WHAT DO I *CALL* YOU?

ME? I'M CAPTAIN AMERICA.

IT WAS MY SECOND TIME MEETING A LIVING LEGEND BUT THIS TIME I KNEW WHAT IT MEANT...

THAT THE WORLD HAD ALREADY CHANGED AGAIN, WE JUST HADN'T NOTICED YET.

The Marvels Project # 6 Cover by Steve Epting

The Marvels Project # 6 Variant Cover by Steve McNiven

PART SIX

NONE OF US KNEW IT AT THE TIME, BUT THE SUMMER OF 1941 WAS A SEASON OF HUNTERS.

FIRST THERE WAS *PRINCE NAMOR*...

WHO'D BEEN STALKING THE STREETS OF NEW YORK IN DISGUISE...

HOPING TO FIND THE *FLAMING MAN* WHO HAD DONE HIM WRONG.

HE HELD TIGHTLY TO HIS HATRED OF *SURFACE-WORLDERS*, EVEN WHEN HE FELT IT FALTERING...

SPARE A DIME, BROTHER?

I'M NOT YOUR *BROTHER*, FOOL.

BECAUSE IT WAS ANGER THAT KEPT HIM STRONG, KEPT HIM SEARCHING.

BUT THE HUMAN TORCH WAS ON A QUEST OF HIS *OWN* THOSE MONTHS, TOO.

SINCE HIS VERY PUBLIC BATTLE WITH NAMOR, HIS LIFE HAD *TRANSFORMED.*

HE WAS NOW ACCEPTED AS A HERO OF THE PEOPLE.

STRIKING OUT IN HIS *TRUE FORM* AT MOBSTERS...

...AS WELL AS THE NEW *COSTUMED* CROOKS WHO'D BEGUN TO APPEAR...

...HE NO LONGER FELT THE *NEED* TO BE A POLICEMAN.

HE UNDERSTOOD WHAT *JUSTICE* WAS, AND HOW TO DELIVER IT.

BUT WHAT HE STILL DID NOT UNDERSTAND WAS THE *HUMANITY* HE FELT INSIDE.

HOW COULD A MAN BUILT IN A LABORATORY EVER FEEL *TRULY* HUMAN?

HAD PROFESSOR HORTON INSTILLED HIM WITH A *SOUL?*

OR WAS THAT SIMPLY ANOTHER NAME FOR THE VERY *SPARK* OF LIFE?

SO HE RETURNED TO THE PLACE OF HIS BIRTH LOOKING FOR ANSWERS...

UNFORTUNATELY, THE PROFESSOR WAS *LONG GONE.*

ALL THAT WAS LEFT WERE SCRAPS OF MACHINERY MEANT FOR A BETTER WORLD.

BUT AMONG THE DEBRIS WAS A *PHOTO* OF THE MAN HE THOUGHT OF AS HIS FATHER... AND HIS *ASSISTANT*...

FRED RAYMOND... OKAY...

...MAYBE *HE'LL* KNOW WHERE TO FIND YOU, PROFESSOR...

HORTON and FRED RAYMOND 1933

BUT AT THE RAYMONDS' STATEN ISLAND HOME, HE FOUND NO ANSWERS...

OH MY GOD...

I *REMEMBER* YOU...YOU WERE THERE MY FIRST DAY...

YOU CAN'T-- YOU *CAN'T* BE HERE!

WE HAVE ENOUGH TROUBLE ALREADY...

WAIT, *PLEASE*...

I DIDN'T MEAN TO BRING *ANY* TROUBLE AT ALL...

I'M JUST SEARCHING FOR THE PROFESSOR...

I HAVEN'T HEARD FROM HORTON IN *YEARS*...

NOW PLEASE...JUST FLY AWAY...

WHAT TROUBLE ARE YOU IN? CAN I *HELP?*

IT'S NOT LIKE THAT...IT'S MY *WIFE*...SHE'S SICK...

IF THE GOVERNMENT FINDS OUT YOU'VE *BEEN* HERE, THEY'LL WANT TO QUESTION ME AGAIN...

AND I *CAN'T* BE SEPARATED FROM HER...NOT NOW...

I'M SORRY...I'LL GO...

FREDDIE! FREDDIE, COME *QUICK!*

NORA?! WHAT--

OH GOD, NO...

...TORO!

MOM...DAD? IT DOESN'T HURT...

WHAT'S *HAPPENING* TO ME?

NO...DID I DO THIS? HOW--

GET OUT OF HERE!

GO-- DAMN YOU!

IT HAD BEEN A LONG TIME SINCE JIM HAMMOND HAD FELT MORE *MONSTER* THAN *MAN.*

BUT THE NIGHT HE MET *TORO RAYMOND,* HE FLEW FAST AND FAR... FULL OF FEAR.

LIKE A *ROCKET* TRYING TO ESCAPE ITSELF.

OVER IN EUROPE, THOUGH, JOHN STEELE HAD BEEN ON HIS OWN DANGEROUS TRAIL...

...IN STEADY PURSUIT OF HITLER'S PERSONAL MONSTER, THE *RED SKULL*.

HE'D SPENT THE SPRING MONTHS SLOWLY CROSSING INTO GERMANY...

...FIGHTING NAZIS WHERE HE FOUND THEM...

...ULTIMATELY ARRIVING AT A FACILITY MUCH LIKE THE ONE HE'D ESCAPED FROM THE PREVIOUS YEAR.

WAS *THIS* WHERE THE RED SKULL WOULD BUILD MORE HORRORS FOR THE WAR EFFORT?

WHAT ARE YOU *DOING* IN THERE, YOU BASTARD...?

WAIT! THIS IS A MISTAKE!
IT'S NO MISTAKE, PROFESSOR SCHMITT... YOUR MOTHER IS A JEW...
...A FACT YOU FAILED TO DISCLOSE TO YOUR SUPERIORS.
SO NOW YOU'LL SEE WHAT IT IS WE DO WITH SPIES AND TRAITORS...
TAKE HIM AWAY.
NO! PLEASE!
MY GOD...ERIC WAS A JEW? I HAD NO IDEA.
I TRUST YOUR EXPERIMENTS CAN PROCEED WITHOUT HIM, PROFESSOR BRUDER?
OF COURSE, HERR SKULL...OF COURSE...

PLEASE... NO...DON'T DO THIS TO ME...

SHUT YOUR *MOUTH,* JEW!

KRAK

YOU CAN DO YOUR TALKING WHEN YOU GET TO THE CAMPS...

GRRROPP

--PROGRESS THUS FAR HAS BEEN *UNACCEPTABLE*...

FORGIVE US, HERR SKULL...THERE HAVE BEEN MANY SETBACKS.

I'M AWARE... WHICH IS WHY I'VE BROUGHT A FRIEND TO HELP YOU...

THIS IS THE ONE WHO INFORMED US WHERE THE *UNDERSEA PEOPLE* COULD BE FOUND...

WE HAVE A *NEW PLAN* YOU WILL HELP US WITH...ISN'T THAT *CORRECT*, MERANNO?

IT *IS*, FRIEND SKULL...

...AND BETWEEN US, WE'LL LEAVE *ALL* OUR ENEMIES IN RUINS...

STARTING WITH YOUR HATED *UNITED STATES*.

BLUE SKIN...? WHAT THE HELL *IS* THAT THING?

IT TOOK A FEW DAYS AFTER HIS TRAGIC FIRST MEETING WITH THE RAYMONDS...

...BUT THE HUMAN TORCH'S FEAR HAD FINALLY BEEN REPLACED WITH *QUESTIONS.*

HOW COULD HIS VERY *PRESENCE* HAVE CAUSED TORO RAYMOND TO *CATCH FIRE?*

WHY DID HE NOT *FEEL* THE FLAMES? WAS THE BOY LIKE *HIM?*

APPARENTLY PROFESSOR HORTON'S EXPERIMENTS HAD FURTHER-REACHING CONSEQUENCES THAN HE'D *IMAGINED.*

HE KNEW HE'D HAVE TO *RETURN* TO THAT UNHAPPY HOME IF HE HOPED FOR ANSWERS...

...BUT IT WOULDN'T BE *THIS* DAY.

IN THE MONTHS SINCE HIS DEFEAT AT CONEY ISLAND, PRINCE NAMOR HAD LOST *TOO MUCH.*

HIS CRUMBLING EMPIRE HAD FACED *INTERNAL REBELLION* AND *BOMBARDMENT* FROM ABOVE.

ALL THOSE LOSSES SCREAMED INSIDE HIM AS HE CHASED THE *TARGET* OF HIS ANGER.

AND HE WAS LIKE A WILD ANIMAL...

RAAAAAAHH!

WHAT--?

WHUU--

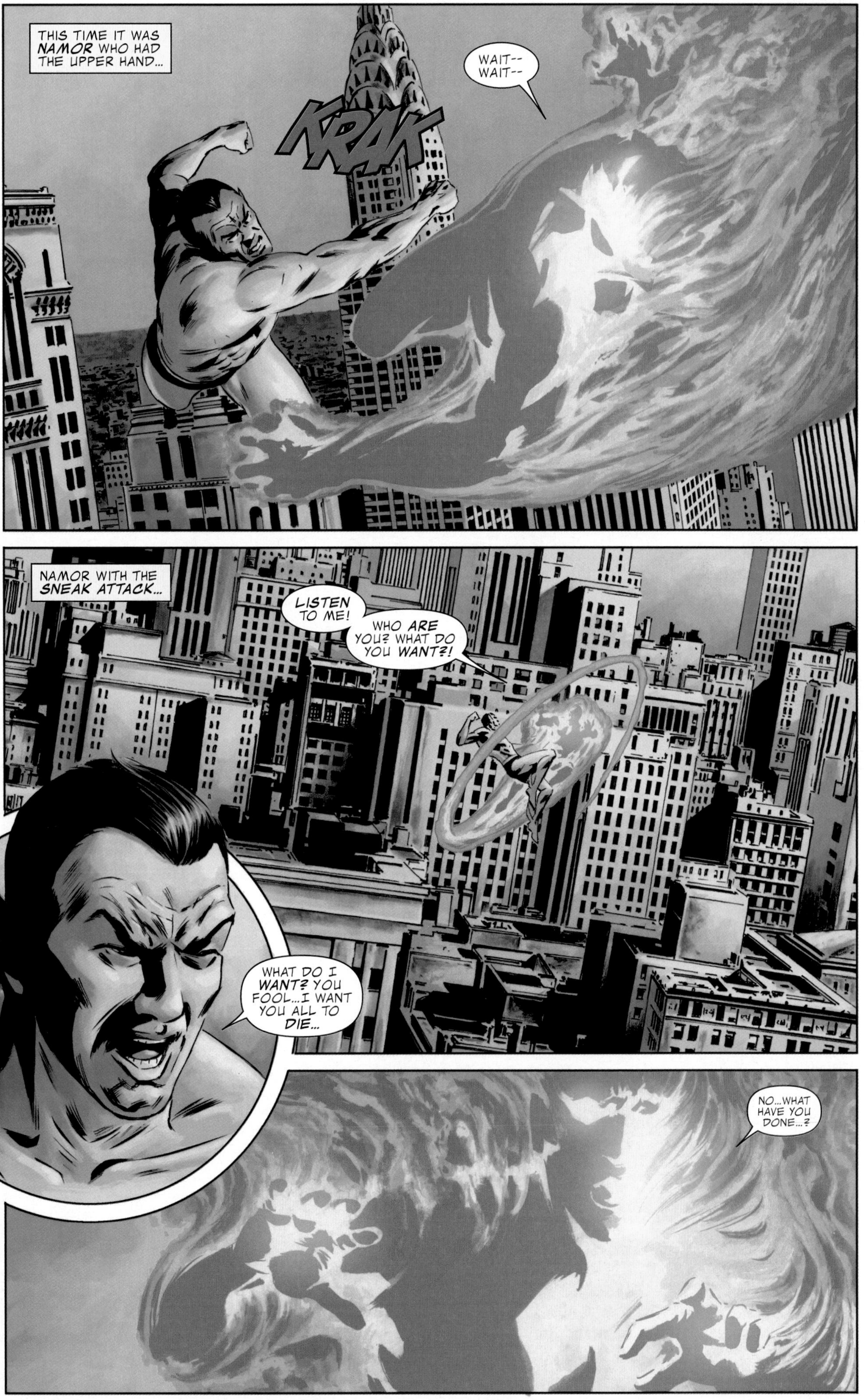
THIS TIME IT WAS NAMOR WHO HAD THE UPPER HAND...
KRAK
WAIT-- WAIT--
NAMOR WITH THE SNEAK ATTACK...
LISTEN TO ME!
WHO ARE YOU? WHAT DO YOU WANT?!
WHAT DO I WANT? YOU FOOL...I WANT YOU ALL TO DIE...
NO...WHAT HAVE YOU DONE...?

AND NAMOR WHO HAD *PREPARED* FOR THIS BATTLE FOR *MONTHS*...

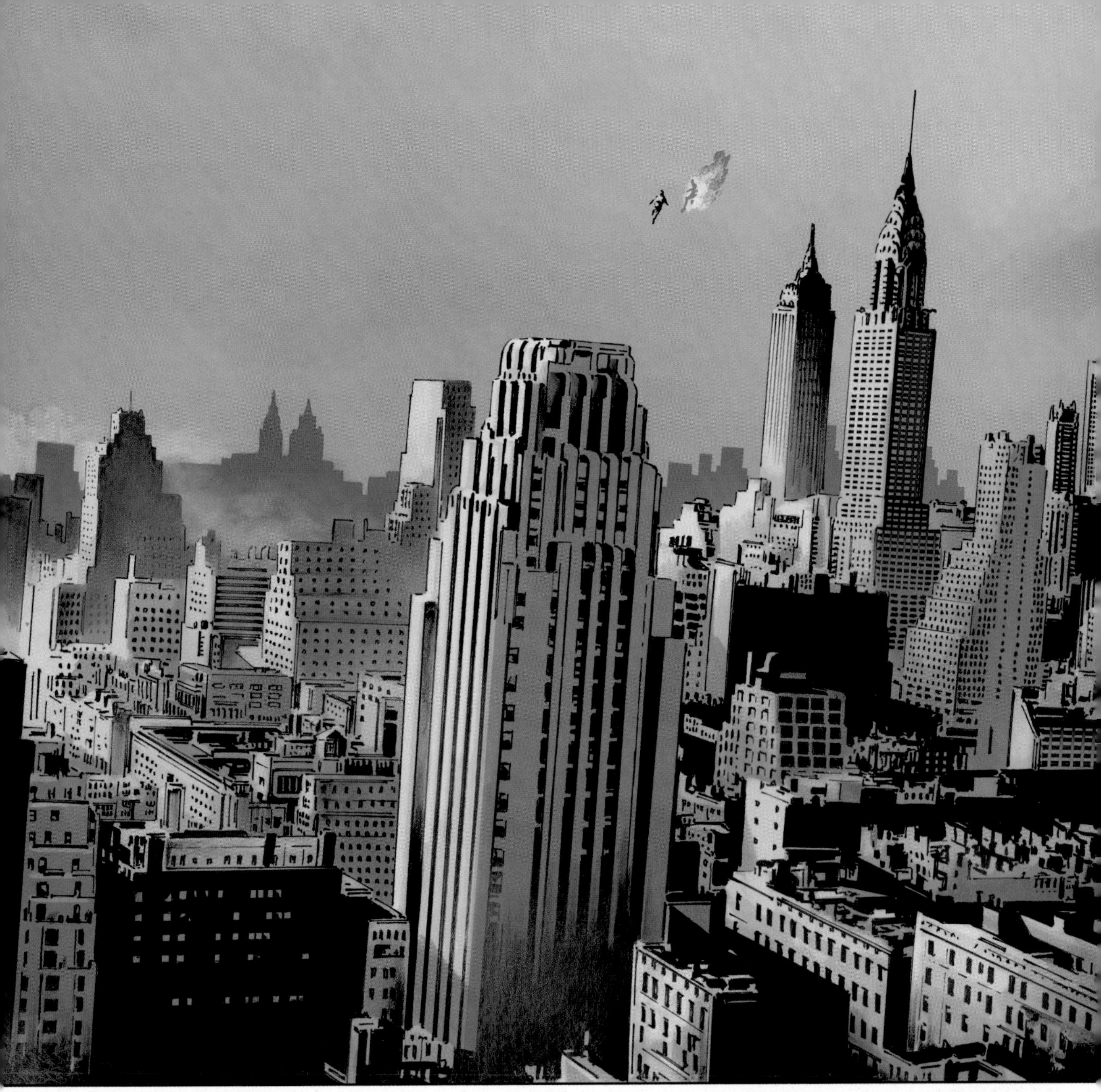
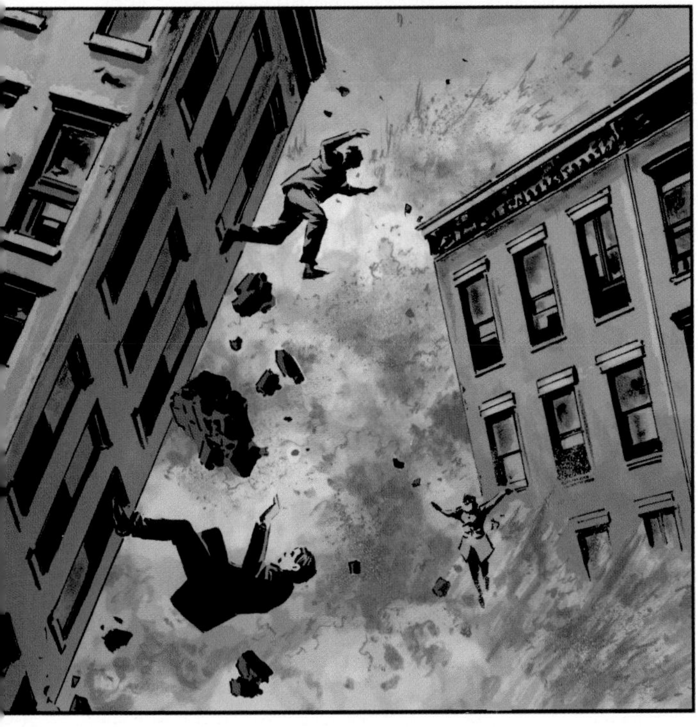
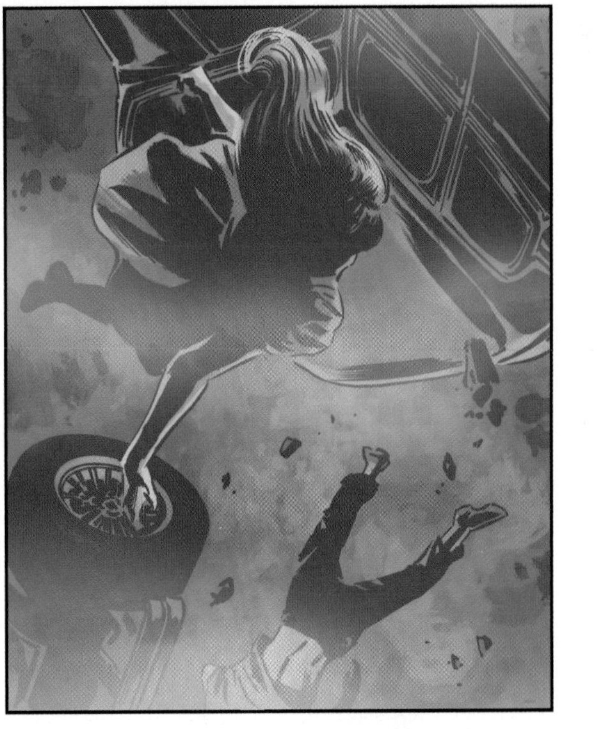

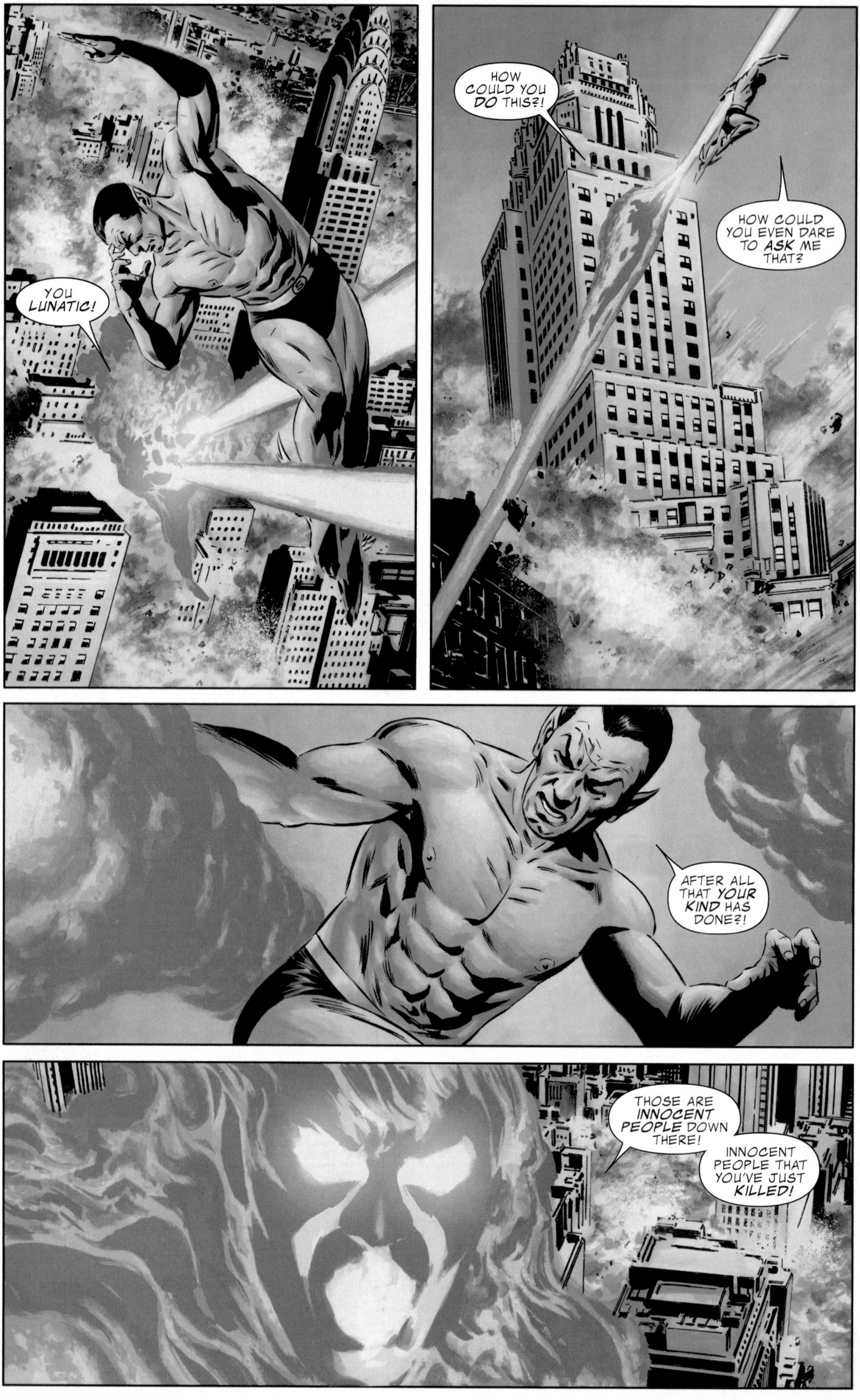
YOU LUNATIC!
HOW COULD YOU DO THIS?!
HOW COULD YOU EVEN DARE TO ASK ME THAT?
AFTER ALL THAT YOUR KIND HAS DONE?!
THOSE ARE INNOCENT PEOPLE DOWN THERE!
INNOCENT PEOPLE THAT YOU'VE JUST KILLED!

YOU KNOW NOTHING ABOUT INNOCENT DEATHS!

NOTHING!

KA-WHAAAAM

AAAAAHH!

YOU WON'T TAKE ME THAT EASILY AGAIN!

MUCH LATER, NAMOR TOLD ME THAT ON THAT DAY, HE THOUGHT ONLY OF HIS KINGDOM, HIS PEOPLE.

HE COULDN'T ALLOW HIMSELF TO CARE ABOUT THOSE DYING BELOW...

HE STAYED HIGH ABOVE, SO WE WERE NOTHING BUT MINNOWS IN THE SEA.

BUT DOWN IN THOSE WATERS, I SAW NEW YORK'S *HERO COMMUNITY* WITNESSING ITS FIRST *TRUE* CALL TO ARMS.

THERE WERE HEROES I'D MET, AND SOME I NEVER SAW BEFORE OR AGAIN.

I KNOW MOST OF US FELT *TINY* IN COMPARISON TO THE DEVASTATION AROUND US...

...BUT WE DID WHAT WE *COULD*.

AND OCCASIONALLY WE WATCHED THE SKIES...

...HOPING THE TORCH WAS MORE *ROBOT* THAN MAN...

...SO HE WOULDN'T FEEL THE *PAIN* OF THE BEATING NAMOR WAS GIVING HIM.

...OW...

IS THAT *ALL* THE FIGHT YOU HAVE, *FLAMING MAN?!*

IS THERE *NO* SURFACE-WORLDER *WORTHY* TO FACE A *PRINCE OF THE REALM?!*

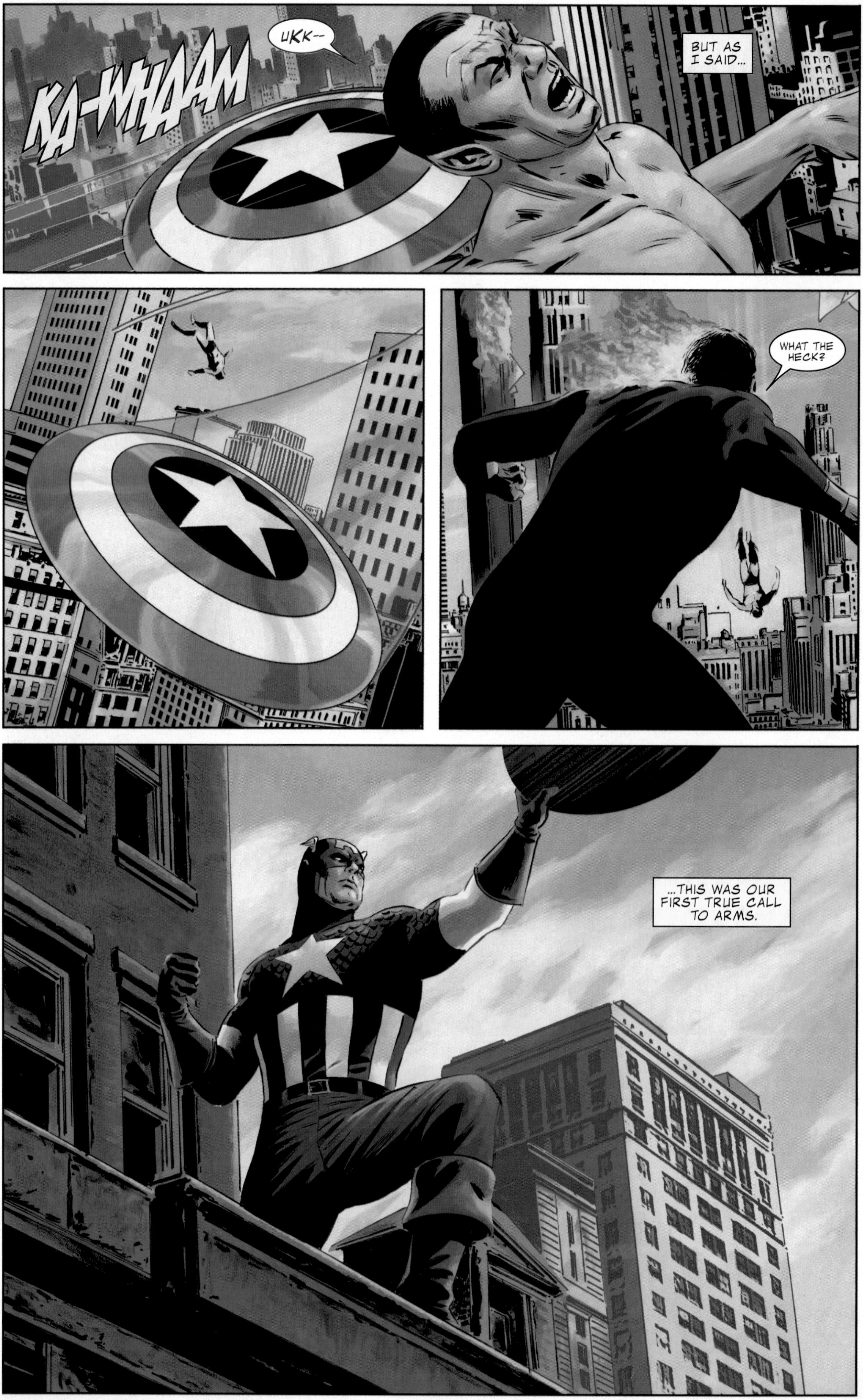
KA-WHAAM
UKK--
BUT AS I SAID...
WHAT THE HECK?
...THIS WAS OUR FIRST TRUE CALL TO ARMS.

SO THERE WAS NO WAY NAMOR COULD HAVE WON THE DAY...

...REGARDLESS OF THE DESTRUCTION HE'D WROUGHT.

AND THE STRANGEST PART OF ALL...

...WAS THAT THIS DAY OF GREAT TRAGEDY WOULD BE THE FIRST STEP...

...TO ANOTHER NEW DAWN.

IS HE DEAD...?

NO, HIS PULSE IS ACTUALLY PRETTY STRONG.

WHICH MAKES MY QUESTION EVEN MORE IMPORTANT...

WHO IS THIS GUY?

The Marvels Project # 7 Cover by Steve Epting

PART SEVEN

THE MONTHS PASSED QUICKLY AS SUMMER MOVED TO FALL AND FALL RUSHED TOWARD WINTER.

BUT NEW YORK WAS STILL WONDERING WHAT HAD HAPPENED TO THE MAN WHO BROUGHT THE TIDAL WAVE.

HE HASN'T SAID *ANYTHING?*

NOTHING WORTH *REPEATING.* THE MAN BARELY *EATS,* EVEN.

JUST SITS THERE GLARING AT THE *WALLS.*

SO WE DON'T EVEN KNOW WHETHER THE GERMANS SENT HIM OR NOT?

NO...OUR ASSUMPTION IS HE'S A *FOREIGN* AGENT...

SOME *SUPER-SOLDIER* LIKE YOURSELF...

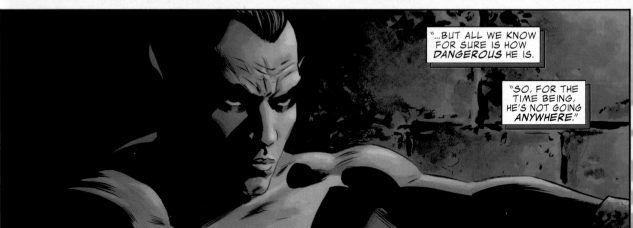

"...BUT ALL WE KNOW FOR SURE IS HOW *DANGEROUS* HE IS.

"SO, FOR THE TIME BEING, HE'S NOT GOING *ANYWHERE.*"

BUT ACROSS THE OCEAN, IN THE DARKEST PLACES, THOSE MONTHS MUST HAVE FELT LIKE *YEARS*.

THE HORROR OF THE NAZI CONCENTRATION CAMPS IS INCOMPREHENSIBLE TO THOSE WHO DIDN'T LIVE THROUGH IT.

ANY DESCRIPTION *FAILS*, EVERY METAPHOR IS TOO SMALL.

IT WAS TO THOSE CAMPS THAT PROFESSOR SCHMITT HAD BEEN *SENT* BY THE RED SKULL...

AND WHERE HE MET A MAN WHO HAD COME TO GERMANY UNDER THE NAME *KEEN MARLOW*... BUT WHO WAS *ACTUALLY* BRIAN FALSWORTH.

NOW, NOW... DRINK IT *SLOWLY*...

FALSWORTH'S FATHER HAD BEEN A MASKED COMMANDO IN THE PREVIOUS WAR, KNOWN AS UNION JACK...

AND FALSWORTH HAD COME TO GERMANY *UNDERCOVER*, ONLY TO BE BETRAYED BY A SOURCE AND *CAPTURED*.

PROFESSOR SCHMITT, THOUGH, HAD SPENT HIS *SEASON IN HELL* SNEAKING INTO THE *EXPERIMENTAL WING*...

HE TRIED AS HARD AS POSSIBLE TO IGNORE THE SIGNS OF TORTURE AND TERROR ALL AROUND HIM...

AS HE WORKED ON A RUDIMENTARY VERSION OF THE *FORMULA* HE'D BEEN STUDYING FOR THE GERMANS.

HE'D HAVE *VENGEANCE* ON THE NAZIS, AND BRIAN FALSWORTH WOULD *BE* THAT VENGEANCE.

UKK... OH, GOD... WHAT...

EASY...THIS IS GOING TO BE *PAINFUL*, MY BOY...

...BUT WE MUST STAY QUIET...

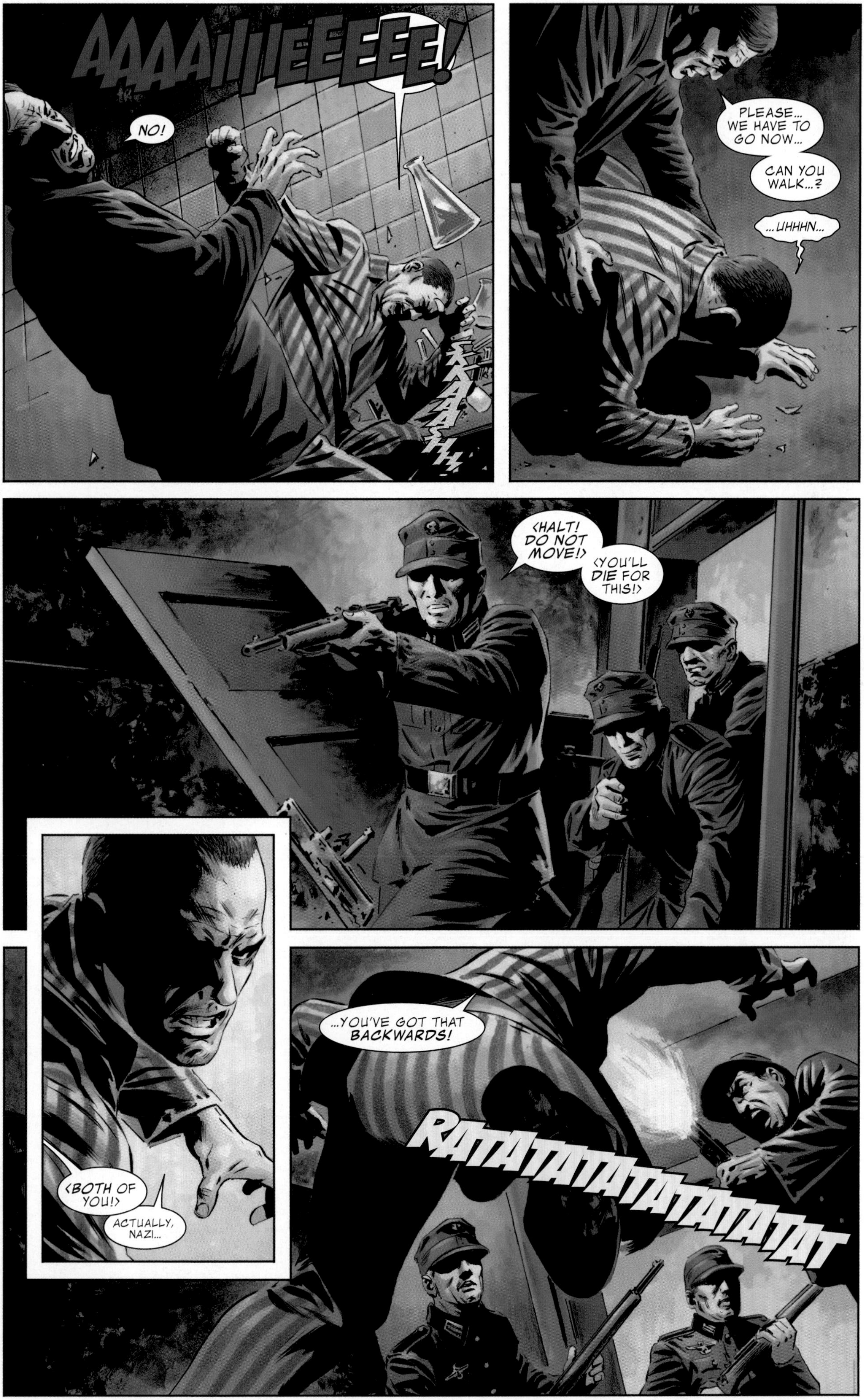
AAAAIIIIEEEEE!
NO!
KKKRAAASHHH
PLEASE... WE HAVE TO GO NOW...
CAN YOU WALK...?
...UHHHN...
‹HALT! DO NOT MOVE!›
‹YOU'LL DIE FOR THIS!›
‹BOTH OF YOU!›
ACTUALLY, NAZI...
...YOU'VE GOT THAT BACKWARDS!
RATATATATATATATATAT

WUHH--

KAA-RAAAAK

RATATATATATATATATAT

PROFESSOR...

IT...IT IS ALL RIGHT... BOY...

...YOU WILL LIVE TO SEE... US ALL...

...AVENGED...

BRIAN FALSWORTH DIED AND WAS REBORN THAT NIGHT...

...THE WORLD'S SECOND CHEMICALLY-CREATED SUPER-SOLDIER.

CREATED BEHIND ENEMY LINES, IN THE VERY MIDST OF THE NAZIS' PUREST EVIL.

HE BURIED HIS FRIEND BEFORE SUNRISE, AND THOUGHT ABOUT HIS DYING WORDS...

AND KNEW THAT SOON HE WOULD RETURN TO THE PLACE OF HIS BIRTH...

...TO SHOW THE NAZIS WHAT HE HAD BECOME...

...A DESTROYER.

BUT FALSWORTH WASN'T THE *ONLY* SUPER-SOLDIER BEHIND ENEMY LINES.

JOHN STEELE HAD ALSO BEEN LIVING IN THE SHADOW OF THE NAZIS.

EVER SINCE HE'D SEEN THE RED SKULL ACCOMPANIED BY A STRANGE MAN WITH *BLUE SKIN*...

...HE'D BEEN *DETERMINED* TO FIND OUT WHAT HITLER'S ENFORCER WAS PLOTTING.

HE FEARED AN OTHERWORLDLY ATTACK WAS BEING PLANNED...

...EXCEPT THIS TIME, HE FOUND THE SKULL MEETING WITH A MILITARY CONTINGENT.

STEELE KNEW THE GERMANS AND JAPANESE WERE ALLIED SINCE THE *TRIPARTITE PACT* THE YEAR BEFORE...

...BUT THIS MEETING WAS *STILL* OUT OF THE ORDINARY, EVEN FOR THE RED SKULL.

FIRST BLUE-SKINNED *FREAKS* AND NOW A JAPANESE *GENERAL* BOWING TO YOU, HUH, SKULL...?

...WHAT THE HELL ARE YOU UP TO?

SO WHILE THE NAZIS WERE ENTERTAINING THEIR *GUESTS* OUT IN THE COURTYARD...

...JOHN STEELE SEARCHED THEIR ANCIENT LAIR FOR *ANSWERS.*

HIS GERMAN WASN'T GOOD ENOUGH TO *READ* THE DOCUMENTS HE FOUND...

BUT HE COULD READ A *MAP* JUST FINE.

AND THE WORDS "WASHINGTON D.C." AND "HAWAII" LEAPT OUT AT HIM.

AMERICA HAD YET TO ENTER THE WAR, BUT THE AXIS POWERS *KNEW* IT WAS ONLY A MATTER OF TIME.

SO THEY PLANNED A *TWO-PRONGED ATTACK* AGAINST THE U.S.

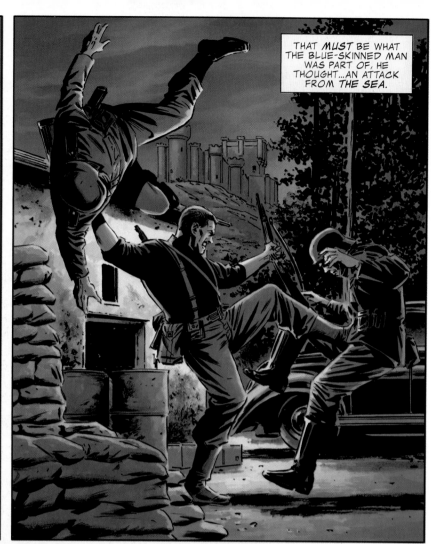

THAT *MUST* BE WHAT THE BLUE-SKINNED MAN WAS PART OF, HE THOUGHT...AN ATTACK FROM *THE SEA.*

JOHN STEELE'S ONLY THOUGHT WAS TO FIND A WAY *OUT* OF GERMANY THAT NIGHT.

TO GET WORD BACK TO *AMERICA...*

...TO WARN HIS COUNTRYMEN ABOUT THESE *INHUMAN* BASTARDS...

WHILE BACK IN AMERICA, AN INHUMAN MARVEL'S LIFE HAD TAKEN A NEW TURN.

LET THE FLAMES *LIFT* YOU, TORO... YOU CAN CONTROL IT *ALL*...

THOMAS "TORO" RAYMOND'S PARENTS HAD BEEN KILLED A MONTH EARLIER IN A *TRAIN CRASH*...

TORO WAS THE *ONLY* SURVIVOR, WHICH HAD BEEN CALLED A MIRACLE.

BUT THE HUMAN TORCH KNEW THE SAD TRUTH...

...THAT THE BOY HAD *SAVED* HIMSELF.

EVEN IN HIS PANIC, HIS POWERS HAD *REACTED* AND *PROTECTED* HIM.

AND THE SYNTHETIC MAN CALLING HIMSELF JIM HAMMOND *KNEW* THAT TORO WOULD BE BLAMING *HIMSELF.*

FOR HIS PARENTS' DEATHS, FOR THE TRAIN CRASH, FOR *EVERYTHING.*

HE'D THINK OF HIMSELF AS A *MONSTER,* UNLESS SOMEONE SHOWED HIM HE *WASN'T.*

AND SINCE HE'D TAKEN TORO UNDER HIS *PROTECTION,* JIM HAMMOND HAD FINALLY BEGUN TO FEEL *TRULY* HUMAN.

NOW HE JUST WAITED FOR WHATEVER THE FUTURE WOULD BRING THEM.

BUT FOR SOME, THAT FUTURE HAD ALREADY ARRIVED...

SO, WHAT'S OUR *MISSION*, CAP?

I'LL TELL YOU ON THE *WAY*, KID...JUST GET *SUITED UP.*

BUCKY BARNES HAD BEEN WAITING SINCE HIS *FATHER* HAD DIED DURING A *FIELD EXERCISE* YEARS EARLIER, LEAVING HIM AN ORPHAN.

RAISED ON MILITARY BASES, BUCKY HAD BECOME THE BASE'S *KID BROTHER*...THEN HE HAD BECOME THE BASE'S *PROBLEM*...

...FIGHTING ALMOST DAILY, WITH SOLDIERS FAR OLDER THAN HIS *SIXTEEN YEARS.*

BUT WITH IMAGES OF THE HITLER YOUTH IN THE NEWSREELS, THE BRASS FOUND A WAY TO *REFORM* BUCKY BARNES...

...*AND* TO COUNTER THE NAZI *PROPAGANDA* MACHINE AT THE SAME TIME.

MONTHS OF *TRAINING* IN THE U.S. AND OVERSEAS IN ENGLAND WITH THE *BRITISH S.A.S.* ...

...AND A *COVER STORY* THAT MADE EVERY AMERICAN KID THINK IT COULD HAPPEN TO THEM...

GEE WILLIKERS! YOU'RE SECRETLY CAPTAIN AMERICA?!

THAT'S CORRECT, *BUCKY*, AND NOW I'LL HAVE TO MAKE YOU MY *PARTNER!*

...AND BUCKY BARNES WAS READY TO FIGHT *SIDE BY SIDE* WITH CAPTAIN AMERICA.

YOU SURE HE'S *UP TO* IT?

YES *SIR*, LIEUTENANT SAWYER...I WOULDN'T HAVE GIVEN THE *OKAY* OTHERWISE.

GOOD TO HEAR...

IF TONIGHT GOES *WELL*, WE'LL HAVE YOU TWO IN FRONT OF THE *CAMERAS* TOMORROW, REENACTING SOME OF IT.

I'M SURE HE'LL *LOVE* THAT...

FOR MY PART, I HAD BEEN ON THE TRAIL OF THE *NAZI SPY MASTER* WHO HAD ESCAPED MONTHS AGO ON THE DOCKS.

AFTER CAPTAIN AMERICA HAD DESTROYED MOST OF HIS RING, HE WENT EVEN *DEEPER* UNDERGROUND.

BUT WHEN HE FINALLY *EMERGED*, ALL THE TIME I'D DEVOTED IN HIS ABSENCE PAID OFF.

MY SOURCES ON THE STREETS AND AT THE DOCKS LED ME *RIGHT* TO HIM...

AND THAT NIGHT I FOUND MYSELF TRACKING HIM *NORTH* OUT OF THE CITY... TO A SECRET MEETING...

I ASSUMED IT WOULD BE MORE NAZI *SPIES* SNEAKING IN BY SEA...

...BUT THIS WAS *NO ORDINARY* MEETING.

AND THESE WERE NO ORDINARY *NAZI* AGENTS.

‹AH, YOU ARE THE *U-MAN,* THEN?›

‹YES, YOUR MASTER, *THE RED SKULL,* SAYS YOU'LL HAVE THE *DOCUMENTS* WE REQUIRE?›

MY PULSE *RACED,* AS I REALIZED I WAS IN *FAR DEEPER* THAN I'D EXPECTED.

AND THEN I HEARD SOMETHING *APPROACHING* IN THE DISTANCE...

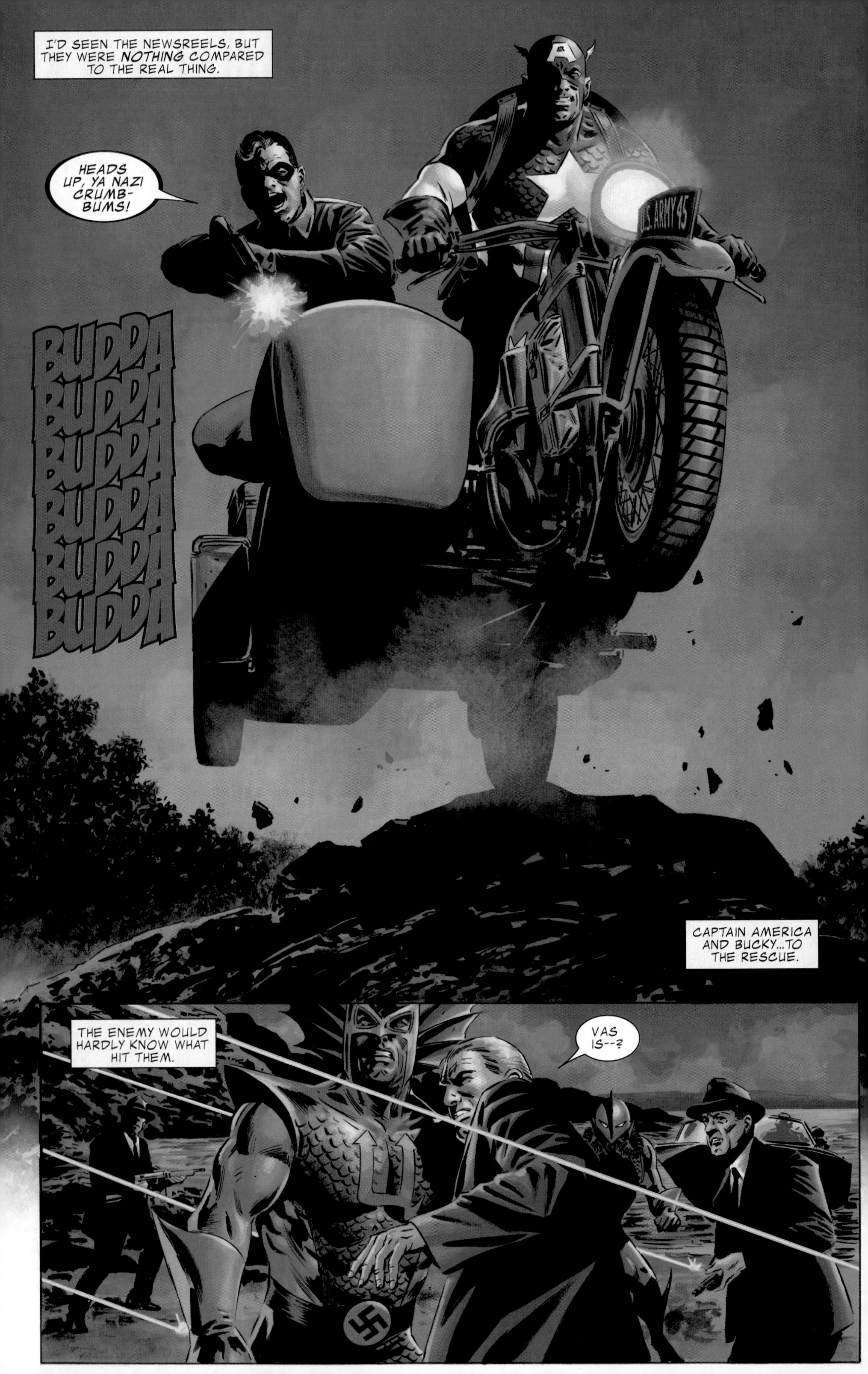
I'D SEEN THE NEWSREELS, BUT THEY WERE NOTHING COMPARED TO THE REAL THING.
HEADS UP, YA NAZI CRUMB-BUMS!
U.S. ARMY 45
BUDDA BUDDA BUDDA BUDDA BUDDA BUDDA
CAPTAIN AMERICA AND BUCKY...TO THE RESCUE.
THE ENEMY WOULD HARDLY KNOW WHAT HIT THEM.
VAS IS--?

LATER, I WOULD HEAR ABOUT THE *WIRES* FROM U.S. AGENTS *ABROAD*.

RAATAAATAAATATATAT

CODED MESSAGES TELLING OF A *SECRET AXIS PLOT* AGAINST THE U.S. THAT HAD LED THEM HERE.

BUT RIGHT THEN, I DIDN'T CARE WHY THEY'D ARRIVED...

FABOOOM

...I WAS JUST *RELIEVED* NOT TO BE TACKLING THIS LOT ON MY OWN.

AHHH!

BLAM BLAMM

HEY! WHO THE HECK--?

EASY, BUCKY...HE'S ON *OUR* SIDE.

NOOOO!

CAP!

DAMNED INTERLOPERS!

UHHN!

BLAM
BLAM
BLAMM

KrAAK

OUT OF THE WAY, NAZI!

CAP!

GET CLEAR OF HIM!

WHUD

NOW, BUCKY! NOW!

BUDDA
BUDDA
BUDDA

AAAIIIEEE!

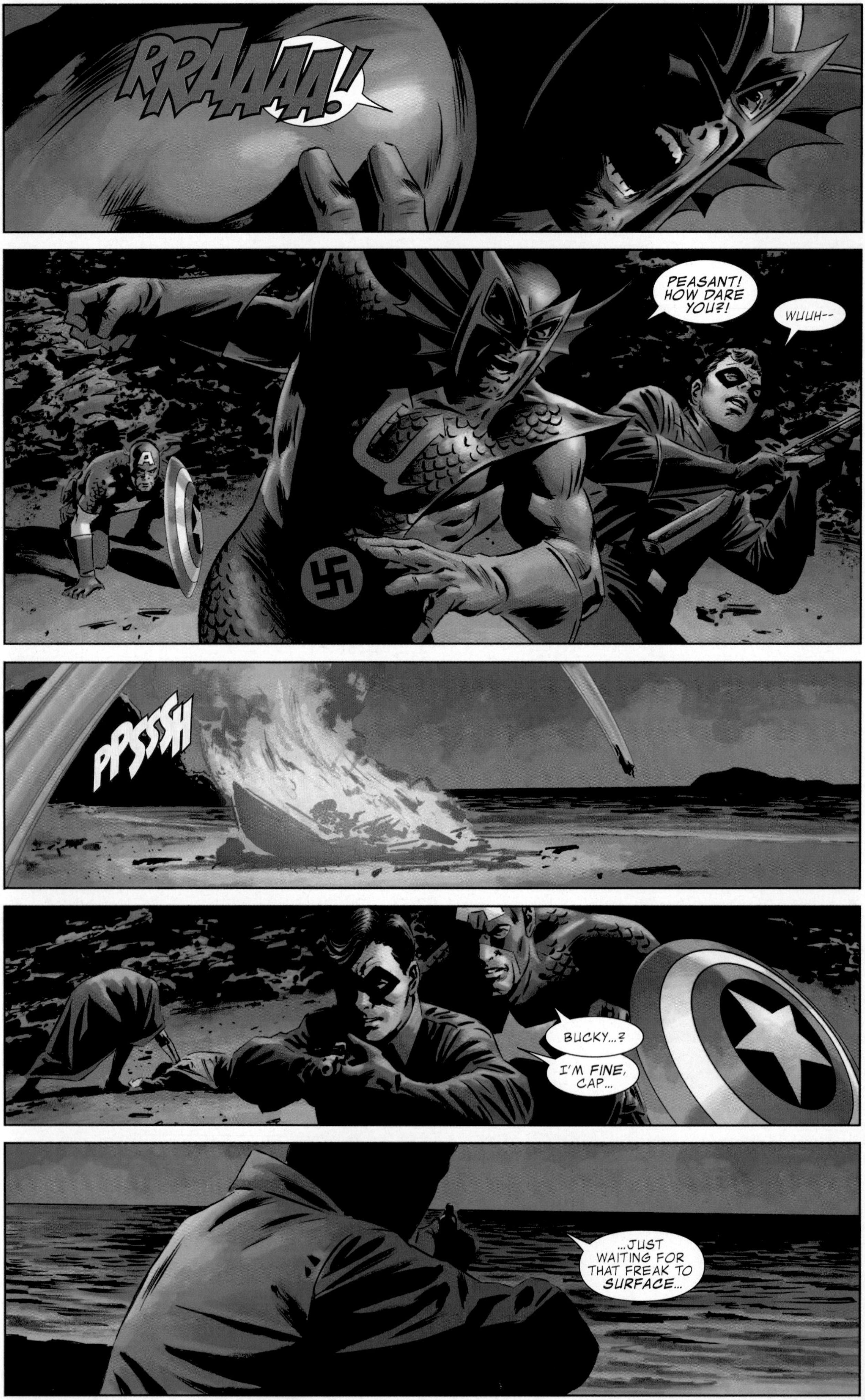
RRAAAAA!
PEASANT! HOW DARE YOU?!
WUUH--
PPSSSH
BUCKY...?
I'M FINE, CAP...
...JUST WAITING FOR THAT FREAK TO SURFACE...

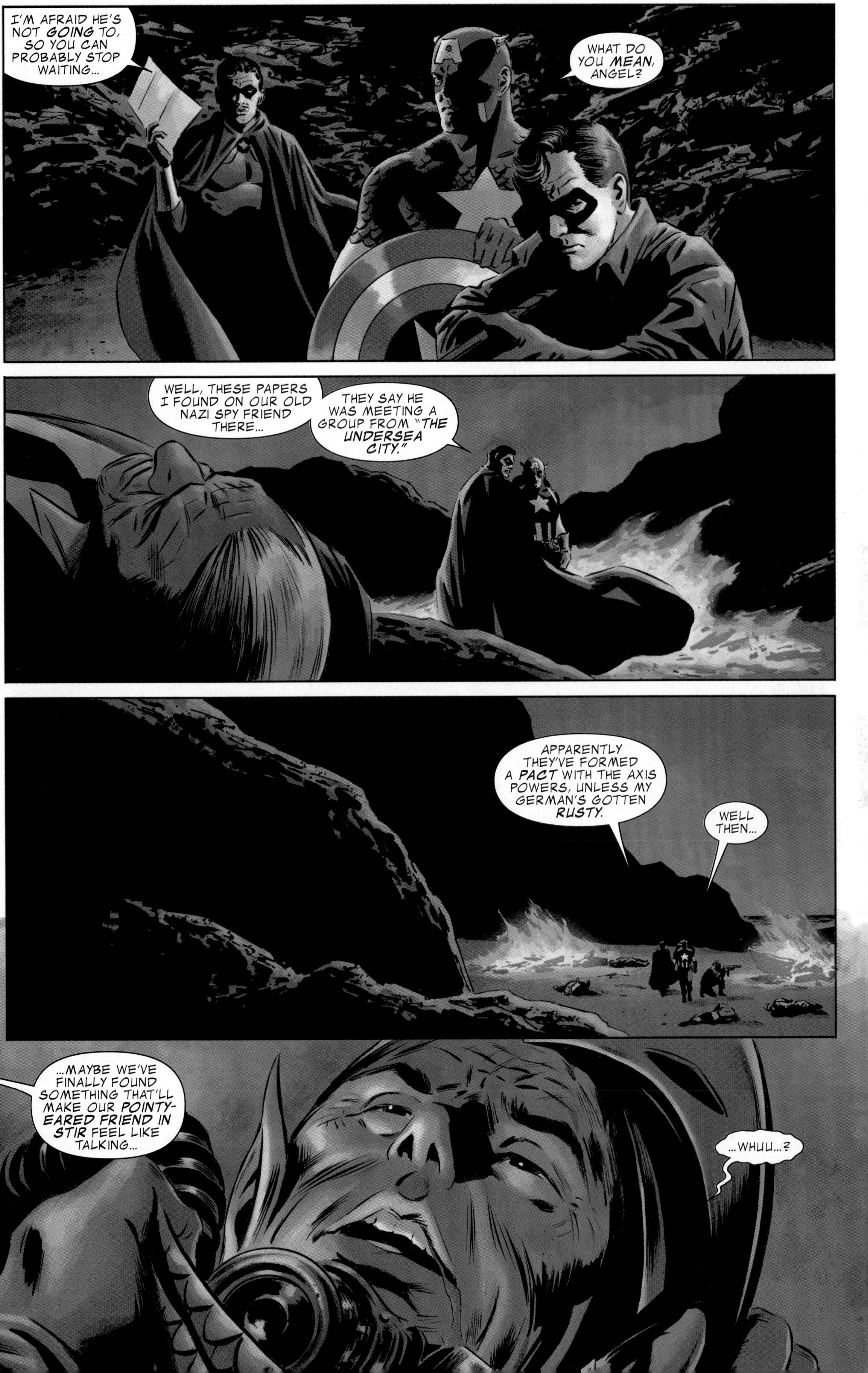
I'M AFRAID HE'S NOT GOING TO, SO YOU CAN PROBABLY STOP WAITING...
WHAT DO YOU MEAN, ANGEL?
WELL, THESE PAPERS I FOUND ON OUR OLD NAZI SPY FRIEND THERE...
THEY SAY HE WAS MEETING A GROUP FROM "THE UNDERSEA CITY."
APPARENTLY THEY'VE FORMED A PACT WITH THE AXIS POWERS, UNLESS MY GERMAN'S GOTTEN RUSTY.
WELL THEN...
...MAYBE WE'VE FINALLY FOUND SOMETHING THAT'LL MAKE OUR POINTY-EARED FRIEND IN STIR FEEL LIKE TALKING...
...WHUU...?

The Marvels Project # 8 Cover by Steve Epting

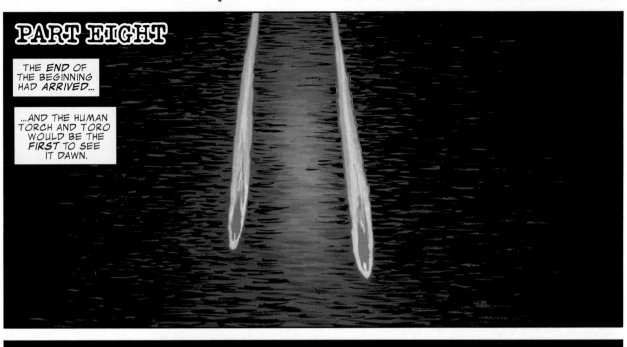

PART EIGHT

THE *END OF THE BEGINNING* HAD *ARRIVED*...

...AND THE *HUMAN TORCH* AND *TORO* WOULD BE THE *FIRST* TO SEE IT DAWN.

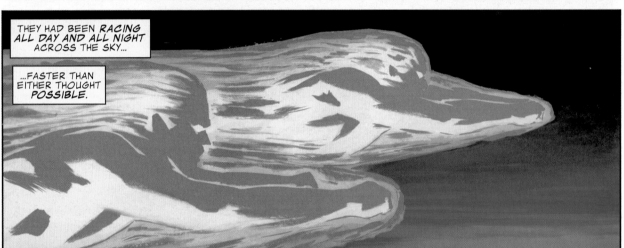

THEY HAD BEEN *RACING* ALL DAY AND ALL NIGHT ACROSS THE SKY...

...FASTER THAN EITHER THOUGHT *POSSIBLE*.

FASTER THAN *JET FIGHTERS*...

...*HURTLING* TOWARDS THE *HAWAIIAN ISLANDS*.

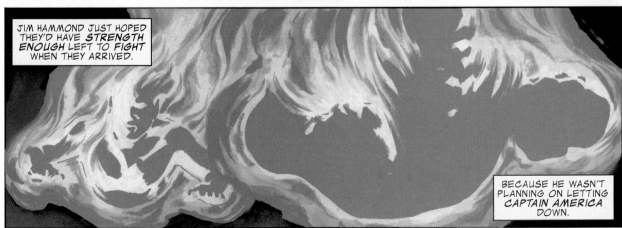

JIM HAMMOND JUST HOPED THEY'D HAVE *STRENGTH ENOUGH* LEFT TO *FIGHT* WHEN THEY ARRIVED.

BECAUSE HE WASN'T PLANNING ON LETTING *CAPTAIN AMERICA* DOWN.

THINGS HAD MOVED *QUICKLY* SINCE CAP HAD TAKEN ONE OF THE UNDERSEA MEN CAPTIVE.

PRINCE NAMOR HAD *FINALLY* DECIDED TO COOPERATE...

...UNDER THE CONDITION THAT *HE* COULD *INTERROGATE* THE PRISONER.

YOU WILL TELL ME *ALL* YOU KNOW, YOU TRAITOROUS *SHARK*...

...OR I WILL CRUSH YOUR *EYES* IN YOUR HEAD.

IT--IT WASN'T *ME*, YOUR MAJESTY!

IT WAS *MERANNO!* HE--HE BETRAYED ATLANTIS!

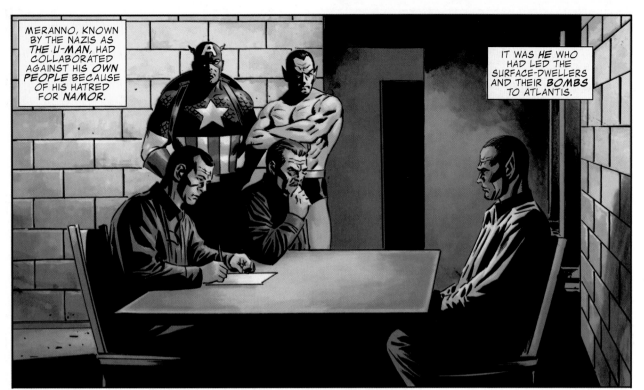

MERANNO, KNOWN BY THE NAZIS AS *THE U-MAN*, HAD COLLABORATED AGAINST HIS *OWN* PEOPLE BECAUSE OF HIS HATRED FOR *NAMOR*.

IT WAS *HE* WHO HAD LED THE SURFACE-DWELLERS AND THEIR *BOMBS* TO ATLANTIS.

NAMOR COULD BARELY *COMPREHEND* IT...

AND AS THE PRISONER REVEALED *MORE* DETAILS OF THE RED SKULL AND U-MAN'S *PLOT* AGAINST THE UNITED STATES...

...WITH THE GERMANS AND SOME OF *OUR* PEOPLE...

...THE PRINCE OF ATLANTIS REALIZED *HOW BADLY* HIS RAGE HAD BEEN *MISDIRECTED*.

AND AT THAT SAME MOMENT, JOHN STEELE HAD *FINALLY* REACHED THE *RESISTANCE* IN FRANCE...

SO HE COULD SEND WORD BACK HOME OF WHAT HE'D *DISCOVERED* IN GERMANY.

I AIN'T GONNA *APOLOGIZE,* SAWYER...I SERVED MY COUNTRY OVER THERE...

I JUST AIN'T BIG ON *FOLLOWIN' ORDERS* LIKE YOU REGULAR ARMY GUYS DO.

SO, IT'S GOOD ENOUGH FOR *RED* BUT NOT YOU, HUNH, *NICK?*

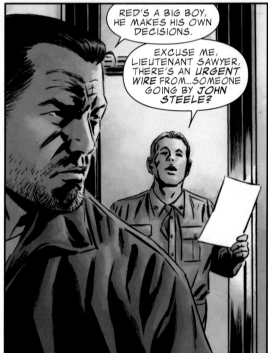

RED'S A BIG BOY, HE MAKES HIS OWN DECISIONS.

EXCUSE ME, LIEUTENANT SAWYER, THERE'S AN *URGENT* WIRE FROM...SOMEONE GOING BY *JOHN STEELE?*

GIVE ME *THAT.*

AW GOD...

GET ME *GENERAL PHILLIPS* ON THE HORN, SOLDIER-- *NOW!*

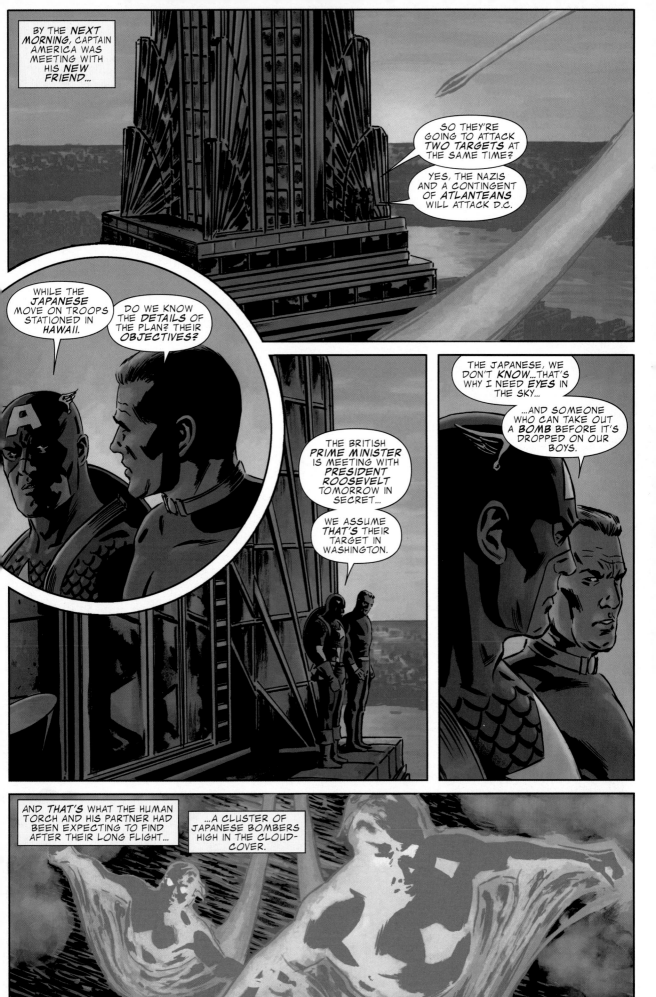

BY THE *NEXT MORNING*, CAPTAIN AMERICA WAS MEETING WITH HIS *NEW FRIEND*...

SO THEY'RE GOING TO ATTACK *TWO TARGETS* AT THE SAME TIME?

YES, THE NAZIS AND A CONTINGENT OF *ATLANTEANS* WILL ATTACK D.C.

WHILE THE *JAPANESE* MOVE ON TROOPS STATIONED IN HAWAII.

DO WE KNOW THE *DETAILS* OF THE PLAN? THEIR *OBJECTIVES*?

THE BRITISH *PRIME MINISTER* IS MEETING WITH *PRESIDENT ROOSEVELT* TOMORROW IN SECRET...

WE ASSUME *THAT'S* THEIR TARGET IN WASHINGTON.

THE JAPANESE, WE DON'T *KNOW*...THAT'S WHY I NEED *EYES* IN THE SKY...

...AND SOMEONE WHO CAN TAKE OUT A *BOMB* BEFORE IT'S DROPPED ON OUR BOYS.

AND *THAT'S* WHAT THE HUMAN TORCH AND HIS PARTNER HAD BEEN EXPECTING TO FIND AFTER THEIR LONG FLIGHT...

...A CLUSTER OF JAPANESE BOMBERS HIGH IN THE CLOUD-COVER.

BUT ON THAT MORNING HE FOUND *SOMETHING ELSE* ENTIRELY...

SOMETHING HE WOULD *NEVER* FORGET.

NO... THIS IS *TOO* BIG...

IT'S *ALL-OUT WAR*...

THIS IS A *MASSACRE*...

WHAT DO WE *DO*, PAPPY?

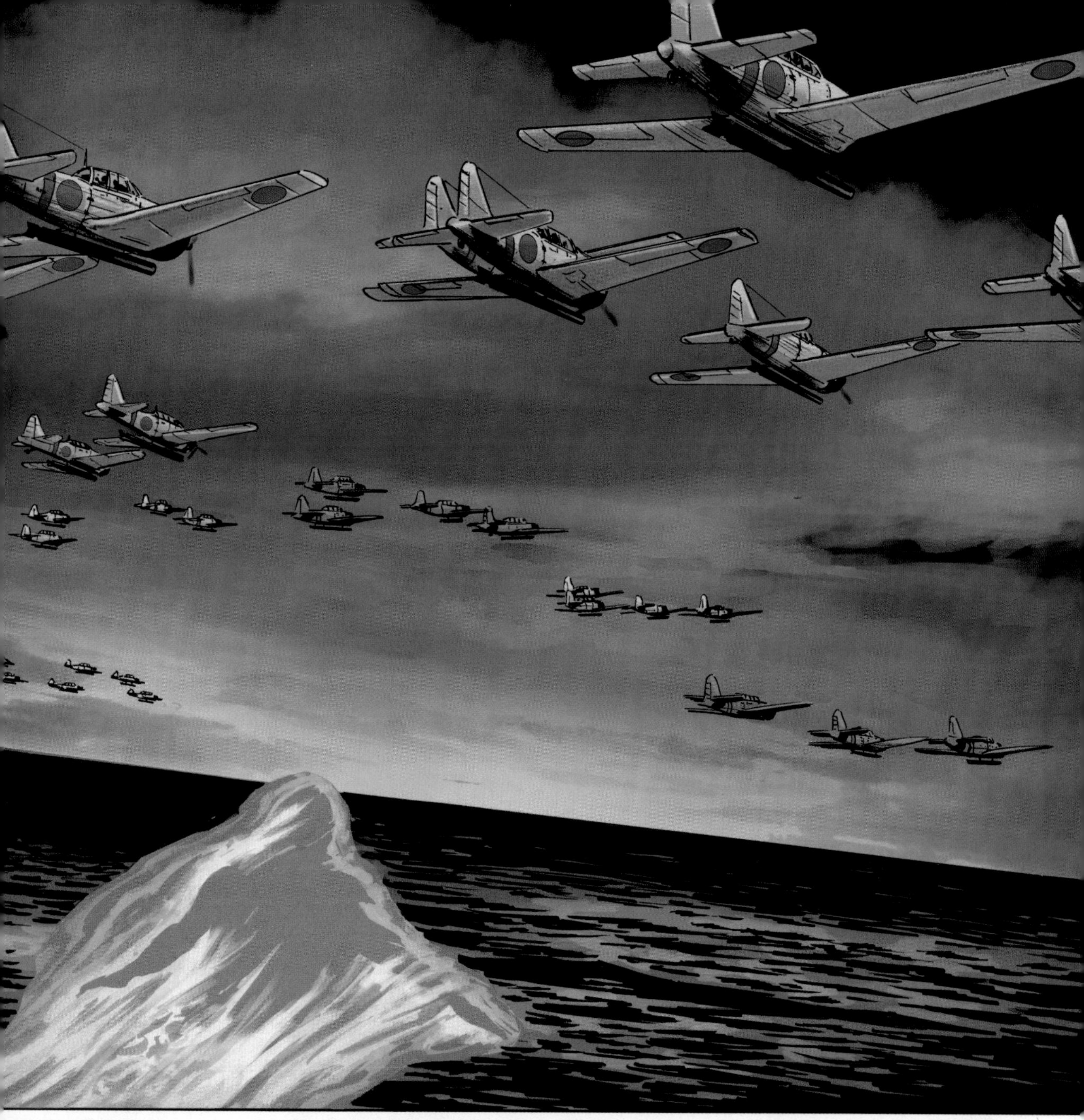

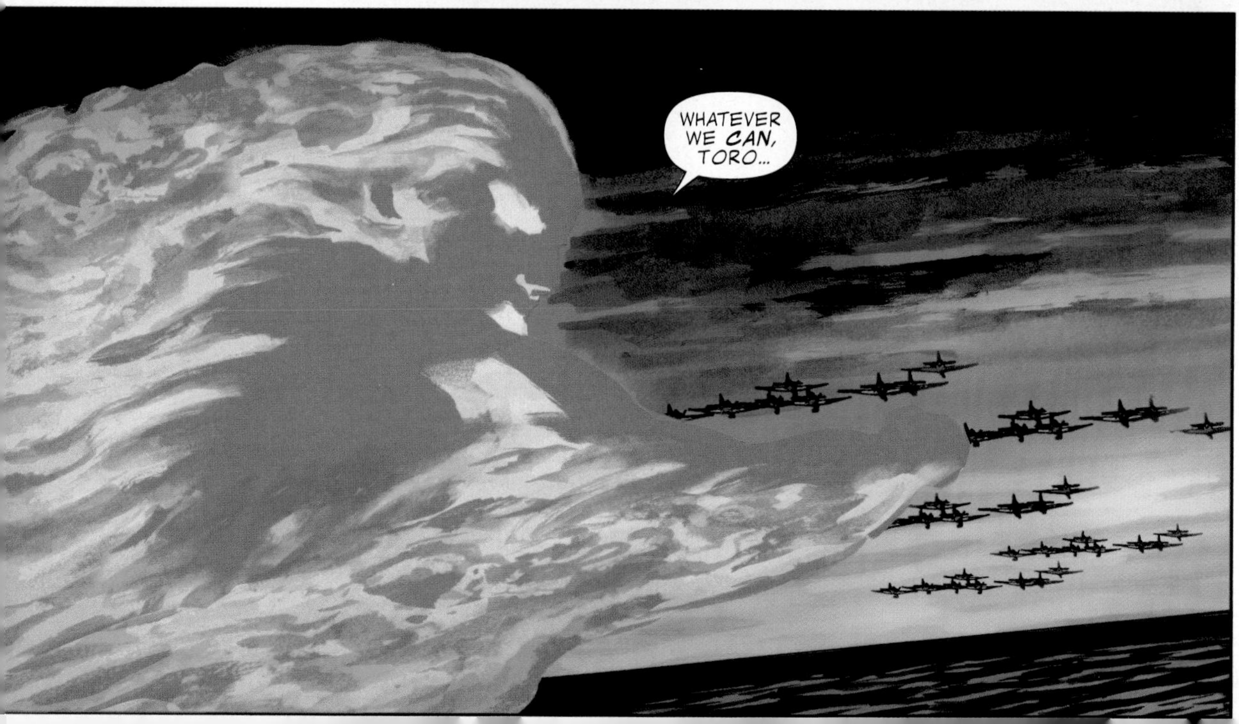
WHATEVER WE CAN, TORO...

AND BACK ON THE OTHER SIDE OF THE WORLD, CAPTAIN AMERICA AND PRINCE NAMOR WERE IN THEIR *OWN* CLOUD-COVER...

...SECRETLY *ESCORTING* THE *BRITISH PRIME MINISTER.*

Y'THINK THEY *CALLED OFF* THE ATTACK, CAP? SINCE WE CAPTURED ONE OF THEIR GUYS?

I HOPE THEY *DID*, BUCKY, BUT I WOULDN'T COUNT ON IT.

THAT'S WHERE WE *DIFFER*, CAPTAIN... I *PRAY* THEY GO THROUGH WITH THIS...

...SO THAT *ATLANTIS* MAY HAVE ITS *VENGEANCE* ON THESE SCUM...

WELL, YOU'RE IN *LUCK*, PRINCE, THEY'RE MAKING THEIR MOVE-- *LOOK!*

OH, I *SEE THEM*, MASKED MAN...

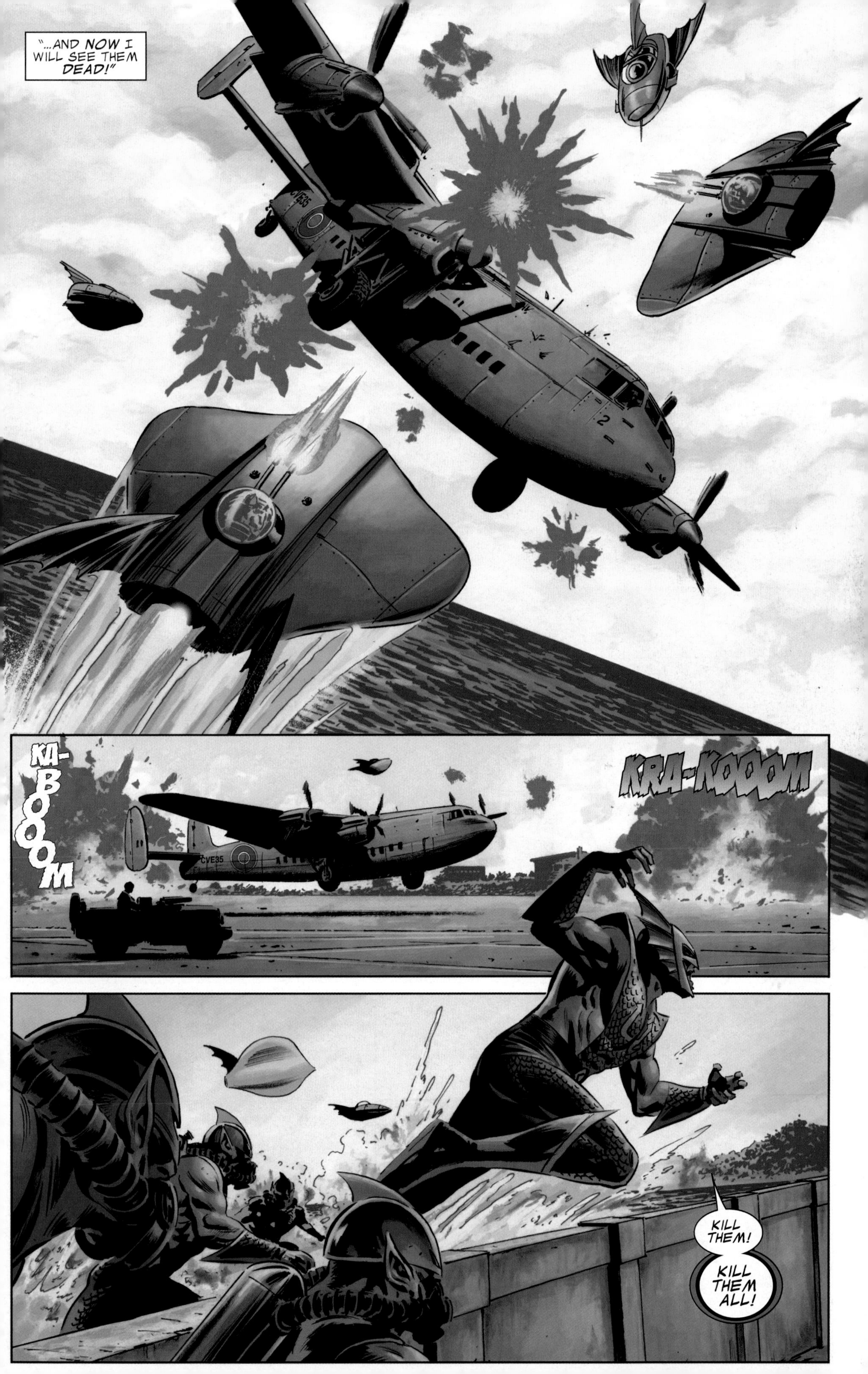
"...AND NOW I WILL SEE THEM DEAD!"
KA-BOOOOM
KRA-KOOOM
KILL THEM!
KILL THEM ALL!

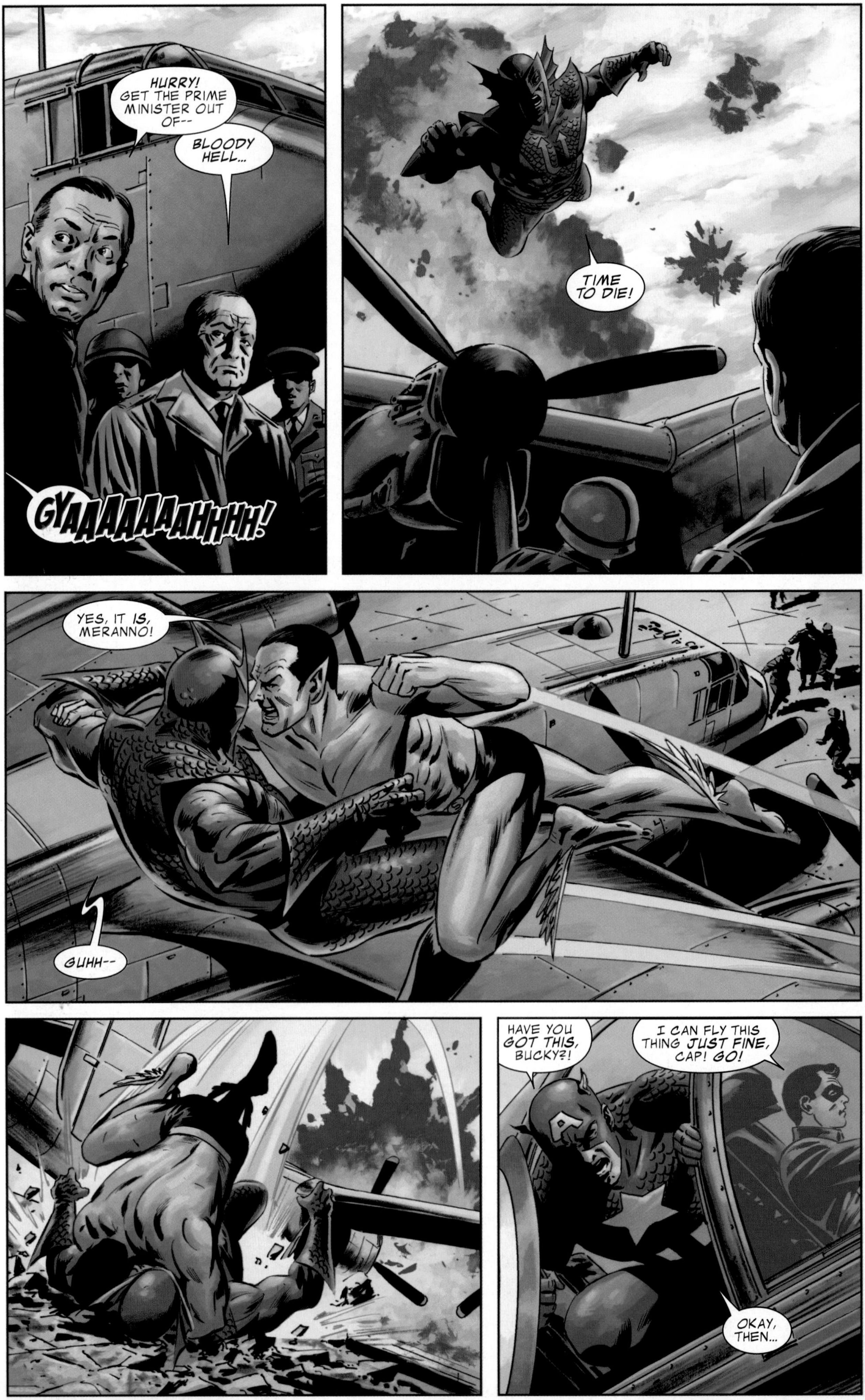
HURRY! GET THE PRIME MINISTER OUT OF--
BLOODY HELL...
GYAAAAAAHHHH!
TIME TO DIE!
YES, IT IS, MERANNO!
GUHH--
HAVE YOU GOT THIS, BUCKY?!
I CAN FLY THIS THING JUST FINE, CAP! GO!
OKAY, THEN...

...SEE YOU ON THE GROUND!

I'D GIVE YOU A CHANCE TO SURRENDER... BUT I KNOW YOU WON'T TAKE IT...

AND SO BEGAN DECEMBER 7TH, 1941...

...WITH *TWO* BATTLES ON *TWO* FRONTS...

ONE FOUGHT IN *PUBLIC* BY SOLDIERS AND DIVE BOMBERS...WHICH WOULD BE A *NATIONAL TRAGEDY*...

AND ONE FOUGHT IN *SECRET* BY MEN IN *MASKS*...MEN WITH STRANGE POWERS...

...AND WARRIORS WHO WOULD HAVE LOOKED *ALIEN* TO OUR EYES.

THAT FIGHT WOULD *REMAIN* SECRET...

...BECAUSE CAPTAIN AMERICA DIDN'T WANT TO *DIMINISH* THE SACRIFICE OF THE MEN AT *PEARL HARBOR*, HE TOLD ME LATER.

THEY WERE THE *REAL* HEROES...THE SOLDIERS WHO BLED AND DIED.

THE ONES WHO DIDN'T HAVE *SCIENCE* ON THEIR SIDE LIKE HE DID.

YEARS LATER, THE HUMAN TORCH WOULD TELL ME OF THIS DAY FROM *HIS* PERSPECTIVE.

HE HAD KNOWN HOW *INHUMAN* MEN COULD BE TO ONE ANOTHER...

...BUT THIS WAS THE FIRST TIME HE WAS EVER *GLAD* NOT TO BE *TRULY* HUMAN.

HE WOULDN'T FEEL THAT WAY AGAIN UNTIL HE SAW THE *NAZI DEATH CAMPS.*

AND A LARGE PART OF HIM WISHED CAPTAIN AMERICA HADN'T *SENT* HIM, OR THAT HE HAD *GONE ALONE.*

BECAUSE HE COULDN'T DO ENOUGH...NO MATTER HOW FAST HE FLEW.

HE FELT LIKE A FIREFLY IN A SWARM OF BEES.

AND HE *HATED* THAT TORO WAS WITNESSING SO MUCH *HORROR* AT SUCH A YOUNG AGE.

SO WHILE CAPTAIN AMERICA AND BUCKY, ALONGSIDE PRINCE NAMOR, *SAVED* THE DAY...

...STOPPED THE *NAZI* AND *ATLANTEAN RENEGADE* PLOT...

...HELPING TO SEAL THE *ALLIANCE* BETWEEN AMERICA AND THE UNITED KINGDOM...

...THE HUMAN TORCH AND TORO FELT *NO VICTORY* THAT MORNING.

THEY SAVED MANY LIVES, STOPPED MANY OF THE JAPANESE BOMBS AND BLEW UP *MANY MORE* OF THEIR FIGHTERS...

BUT THEY COULDN'T HOLD BACK THE STORM NO MATTER HOW HARD THEY TRIED.

IT WAS A *HARD* LESSON, AND IT STUCK WITH JIM HAMMOND FOR THE REST OF THE WAR.

DAMN THEM... DAMN THEM ALL...

BECAUSE FOR AMERICA, THE WAR WE KNEW WAS COMING HAD FINALLY BEGUN.

SO...WHAT HAPPENS *NOW*, CAP?

EPILOGUE

THINGS MOVED SWIFTLY AFTER THAT FATEFUL DAY.

PRESIDENT ROOSEVELT COMMISSIONED AMERICA'S FIRST SUPER-TEAM, CODE-NAMED *THE INVADERS.*

NAMOR WAS *PARDONED* ON THE CONDITION HE BECOME PART OF THIS TEAM.

AND HE SOON FOUND *TRUE FRIENDSHIP* AMONG THE ENEMIES OF HIS ENEMIES.

LED BY *CAPTAIN AMERICA,* THE INVADERS FOUGHT THE WAR ON ALL ITS *FRONTS*...

...AND EVEN *BEHIND* ENEMY LINES.

THEIR EXPLOITS WERE TOLD IN *BOLD PRINT* AND *NEWSREELS.*

NICK FURY WAS NEARLY *DESTROYED* BY THE DEATH OF HIS BEST FRIEND *RED HARGROVE* AT PEARL HARBOR.

BUT HE SURVIVED HIS GRIEF BY LEADING A TEAM OF *ARMY COMMANDOS* KNOWN AS THE *HOWLERS.*

OKAY, AXIS--HERE WE COME!

WAAH-HOOOO!

JOHN STEELE CONTINUED TO FIGHT THE NAZIS ON HIS OWN, IN SECRET...

...UNTIL HE *DISAPPEARED* WITHOUT A TRACE SHORTLY AFTER THE *INVASION OF NORMANDY.*

AND BACK HOME IN NEW YORK, I KNEW THAT THE ERA OLD MATT HAWKINS HAD TOLD ME ABOUT HAD *FINALLY* ARRIVED...

AN ERA OF WAR AND STRIFE AND LOSS, BUT *ALSO* AN ERA OF WONDER AND SCIENTIFIC BREAKTHROUGH...

AN ERA OF *MARVELS*... AN ERA OF *HEROES.*

I STAYED IN MY CITY, FIGHTING MOBSTERS, KILLERS, AND SPIES... AND I WATCHED *OTHER* HEROES COME AND GO...

AND DESPITE EVERYTHING... IT TRULY *WAS* THE GREATEST OF TIMES.

I'M SORRY...I DON'T UNDERSTAND...

YOU'RE JASON *HALLOWAY,* AREN'T YOU?

AND YOUR GRANDFATHER WAS *THOMAS HALLOWAY?*

UM, YES, BUT I NEVER *KNEW* HIM...HE WAS IN HIS *FIFTIES* BY THE TIME MY *FATHER* WAS BORN...

WELL, MY NAME IS *STEVE ROGERS,* AND YOUR GRANDFATHER WANTED YOU TO *HAVE THIS...*

ROGERS? WAIT--*CAPTAIN AMERICA?*

CAPTAIN AMERICA KNEW *MY* GRANDFATHER?

YES...HE WAS ONE OF THE *FINEST MEN* I'VE EVER MET.

MY SOURCES SAY *YOU* TAKE AFTER HIM, WHETHER YOU REALIZE IT OR NOT...

OH...WELL, *THANKS,* I GUESS. HE WAS A GREAT *DOCTOR,* I ALWAYS HEARD.

I'LL SEE MYSELF OUT...JUST WANTED TO MAKE SURE THAT PACKAGE *GOT* TO YOU.

IT WAS AN OLD *PROMISE* I MADE.

WELL... WHAT DO YOU *THINK?*

HARD TO *SAY*...I GUESS ONLY TIME WILL TELL.

TIME... RIGHT.

SO, I INSPIRED HIS *GRANDFATHER?*

NOT YET...BUT SOMEDAY, WHEN YOU'RE *MUCH* OLDER...

WE'RE NOT *DONE* WITH YOU YET, MATT HAWKINS...

WHEN I'M *OLDER,* IN THE *PAST*...

WHAT A *STRANGE* WORLD WE LIVE IN...

WHAT THE HELL...? MASK AND *GUNS?*

AND...?

THE MARVELS PROJECT:
The Early Days of
The Age of Heroes

By Dr. Thomas Halloway

THE END.

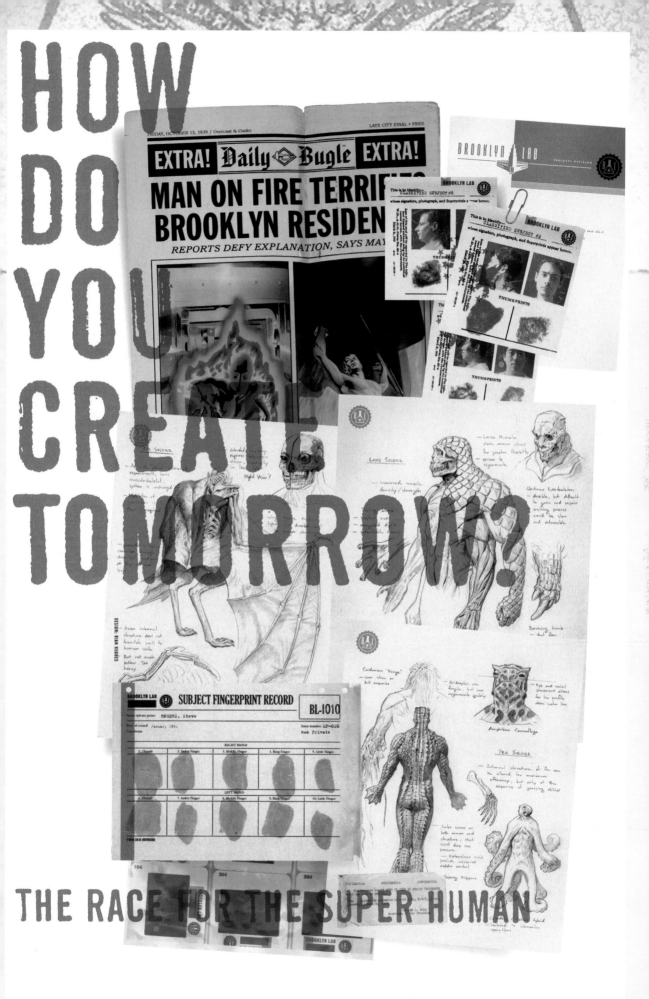

HOW
DO
YOU
CREATE
TOMORROW?

THE RACE FOR THE SUPER HUMAN

HOW DO YOU CREATE TOMORROW?

THE RACE FOR THE SUPER HUMAN

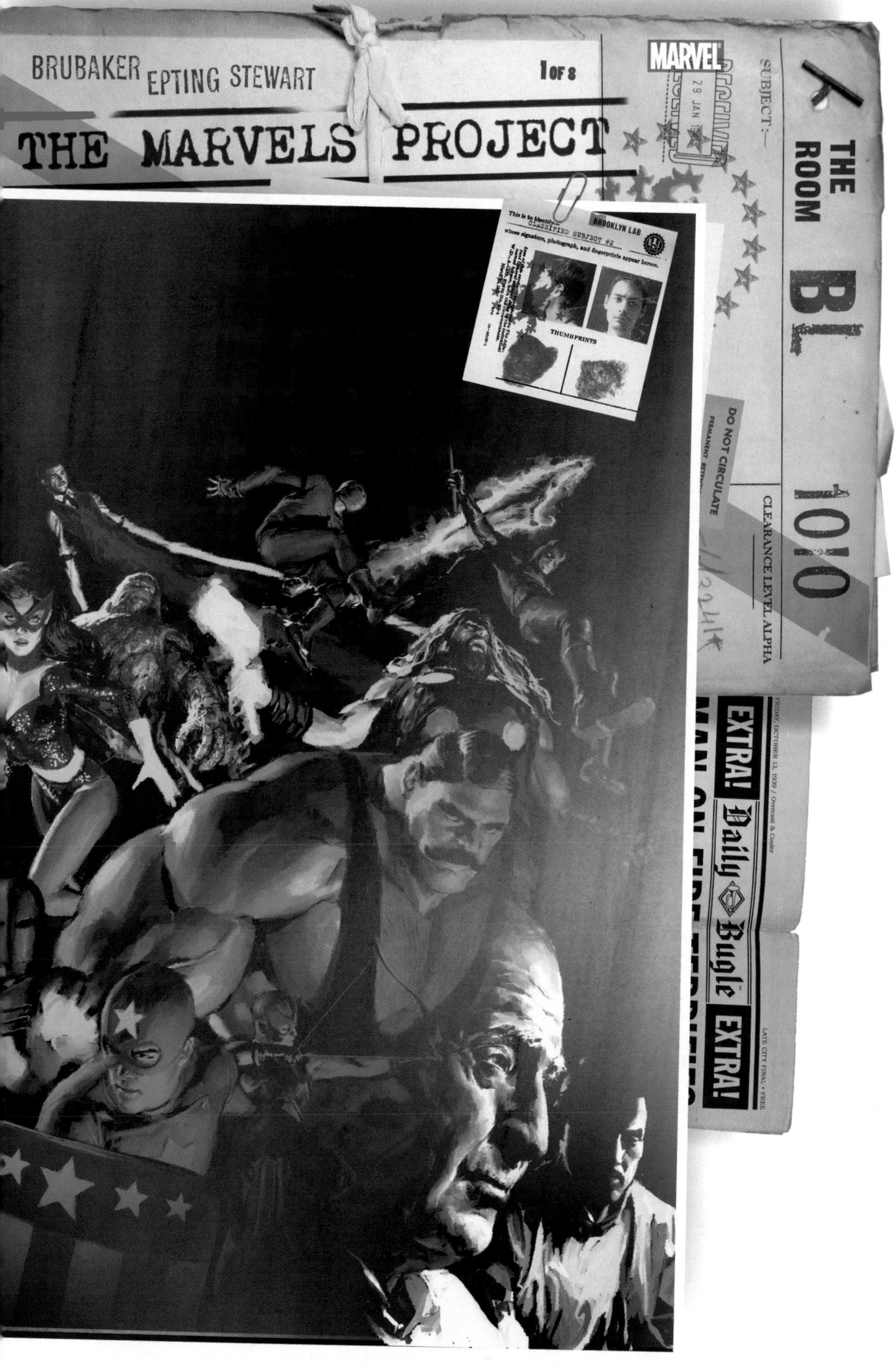
BRUBAKER EPTING STEWART
1 OF 8
MARVEL
THE MARVELS PROJECT
SUBJECT:—
THE ROOM
BL
1010
CLEARANCE LEVEL ALPHA
29 JAN
BROOKLYN LAB
This is to identify
CLASSIFIED SUBJECT #2
whose signature, photograph, and fingerprints appear hereon.
THUMBPRINTS
DO NOT CIRCULATE
FRIDAY, OCTOBER 13, 1939 / Overcast & Cooler
EXTRA!
Daily Bugle
EXTRA!
LATE CITY FINAL • FREE

The Marvels Project # 1 Variant Cover by Gerald Parel

The Marvels Project # 1 Variant Cover by Phil Jimenez

The Marvels Project # 1 Variant Cover by Steve McNiven

The Marvels Project # 1 Sketch Variant Cover by Steve McNiven

The Marvels Project #2 Variant Cover by Steve McNiven

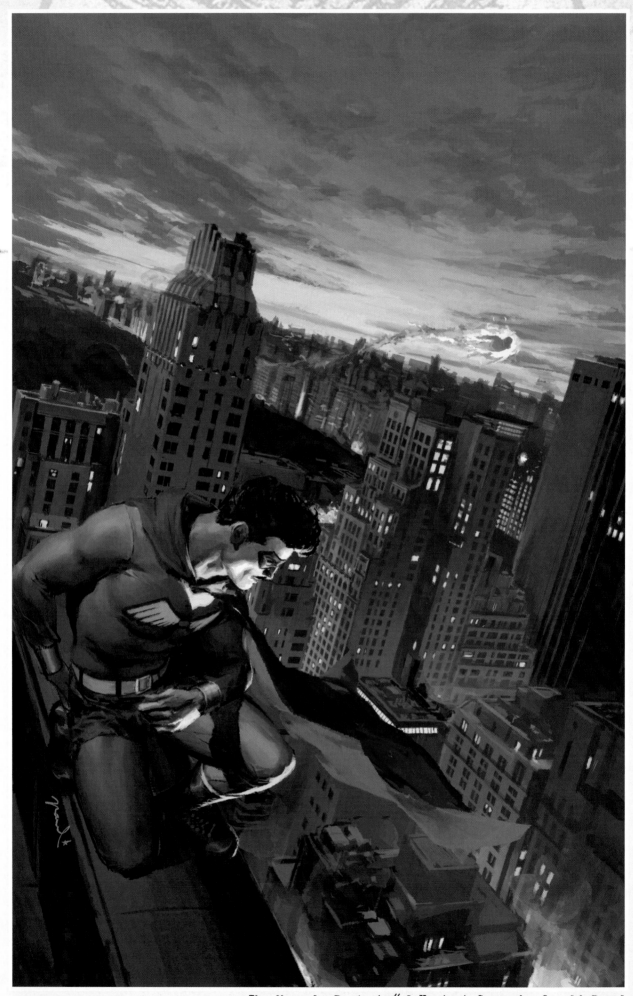

The Marvels Project # 2 Variant Cover by Gerald Parel

The Marvels Project # 3 Variant Cover by Steve McNiven

The Marvels Project # 3 Variant Cover by Gerald Parel

The Marvels Project # 4 Variant Cover by Gerald Parel

The Marvels Project # 5 Variant Cover by Steve McNiven

The Marvels Project # 5 Variant Cover by Gerald Parel

The Marvels Project # 6 Variant Cover by Gerald Parel

The Marvels Project # 7 Variant Cover by Steve McNiven

The Marvels Project # 7 Variant Cover by Gerald Parel

The Marvels Project # 8 Variant Cover by Steve McNiven

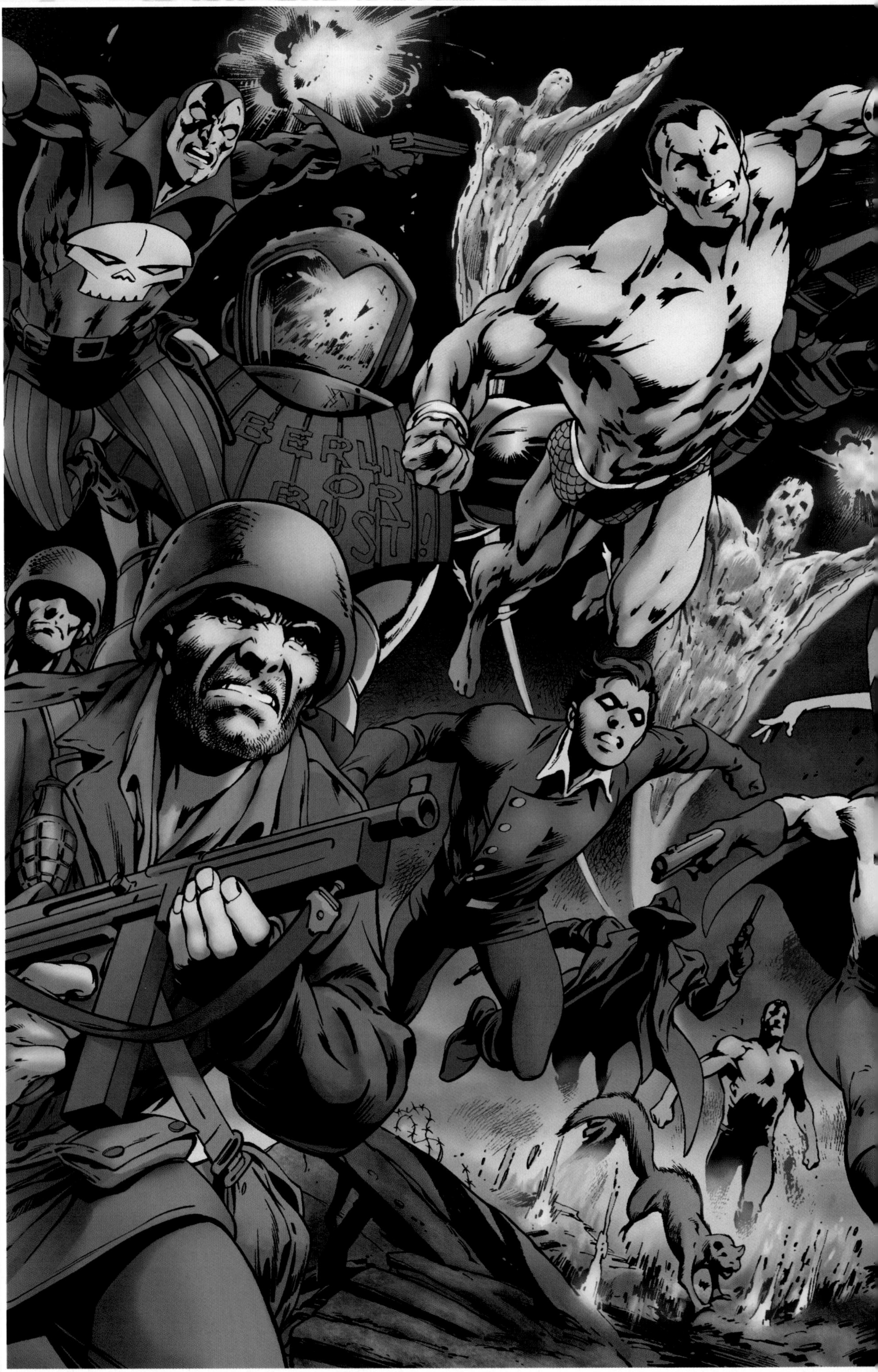
BERLIN OR BUST!

The Marvels Project # 8 Variant Cover by Alan Davis

The Marvels Project # 8 Variant Cover by Gerald Parel

DAILY ❦ BUGLE™

WHO ARE THE MARVELS?

MERE URBAN LEGENDS OR GODS OF MYTHOLOGY LIVING AMONG US?

1939 Daily Bugle Cover by Mike Mayhew

VIOLENT SPREE BY WING-FOOTED, AQUATIC MAN

S.S. RECOVERY SUNK, CAPE ANNA LIGHTHOUSE STORMED

By JOHN RHETT THOMAS – Bugle Staff Reporter

There was mayhem on the North Atlantic high seas and the inshore waters near Long Island's Cape Anna lighthouse, as authorities report a brazen attack upon both ship and shore by a man allegedly at home under water, on the ground, and in the sky. The terrifying encounters were recorded by many, among them the crew aboard the S.S. Recovery and a pilot thrown from the cockpit of a Coast Guard biplane. The identity of the assailant is unknown, but if reports from the witnesses, some of whom lie critically injured in respective hospitals, are to be believed, he was a lone man of astonishing strength and gifted with the power of flight. Strangely, they added, he had a young girl in tow. It is unclear if she is an innocent hostage

or a willing accomplice, but police authorities and available Coast Guard and naval assets are mobilized all along the Atlantic Seaboard.

The intrigue began two nights ago in the waters below the salvage ship S.S. Recovery, positioned near Flat Shoals, southeast of Massachusetts' remote Block Island, when the mutilated dead bodies of two divers were found next to the submerged merchant ship. According to the testimony of the Recovery's Capt. Leonard Johnson, 54, diver Chip Anderson, 32, discovered the bodies of fellow divers Rod Nelson, 37, and Ev Carley, 42, both savagely killed while discharging their duties. Anderson, resting in stable condition with a bad case of the bends, was unavailable for comment.

Aquatic man runs amok after wild melee with Hampton police.

Immediately after the revelation of his diver's bodies, Capt. Johnson's ship was seized by a power of unknown, unnatural origin and dashed upon the treacherous reefs of Flat Shoals.

With his ship sundered in two and mates scrambling to gain the lifeboats, Johnson reported seeing a man clad only in green swim trunks flying above the action, seemingly taking an appraisal of the misery of the Recovery. The man did not give any aid, but plunged into the chilly Atlantic and disappeared.

Shortly thereafter, police in nearby East Hampton, NY responded to an emergency at Cape Anna Lighthouse, where a man of similar description began a rampage of similar destruction. The keeper of the lighthouse, Randall Smith, 72, was viciously assaulted after answering a knock at his door. An arriving police force arrived to witness the flying man, apparently with wings on his feet, continue his violent spree by leaping atop a bi-plane piloted

Story continues in *Golden Age Marvel Comics Omnibus Vol. 1 HC.*

HUMAN TORCH RETURNS, CREATOR MISSING

DR. PHINEAS HORTON POSSIBLE VICTIM OF ANDROID'S FLAME

By DUGAN TRODGLEN – Bugle Staff Reporter

Controversial scientist Professor Phineas Horton has gone missing Wednesday after his home and laboratory burned down, the seeming victim of his own creation, the so-called Human Torch. The artificial human, referred to in scientific jargon as an "android," had been buried deep underground since March after Horton unveiled it to an astonished group of journalists and fellow scientists. An investigation is under way to determine how the android managed to escape. It was believed that Horton was experimenting with ways to control the android's flame and was hoping to one day unearth his creation. The current whereabouts of the Human Torch are unknown, as some witnesses claimed to see it fly off into the night.

In a separate but possibly related incident, the home of alleged crime boss Anthony Sardo also burned to the ground last night, killing Sardo and several others. There are unsubstantiated reports that the Human Torch was in the area and was responsible for the fire, although officers on the scene seemed noncommittal on the subject. If these allegations prove true, the New York City police department may have

a significant crisis on their hands. Some accounts even have the creature resisting the dousing of a fire hose, the water merely steaming off of it. A press conference organized by police officials this afternoon will address the threat of the Human Torch and perhaps clear up some of the fact and fiction regarding this alarming turn of events.

Horton introduced the world to his Human Torch synthetic creation in March, hoping for assistance from the scientific community in discovering the source of and solution to his creation's fatal flaw: When exposed to oxygen, the otherwise astounding feat of scientific accomplishment caught fire and burned in a hot, red flame while somehow remaining "alive." The only response the Professor received, however, was the unanimous call for the android's destruction. Horton compromised, burying the Torch in a supposedly airproof concrete "tomb" near his home.

Little is known about the intelligence of the synthetic being, and its motives are a total mystery. Indeed, some have postulated that the fire, or fires, may have been completely inadvertent, something the Human Torch had no

Firemen attempt to douse fire of so-called Human Torch.

control over, while others insist the creature is a malicious menace bent on destruction, and likely to succeed. Until the Human Torch is found, there can only be speculation regarding

what really happened. Accident or no, however, there appears to be a

Story continued in *Golden Age Marvel Comics Omnibus Vol. 1 HC.*

ANGEL, SCOURGE OF CRIME, GOES ON RECORD

"SIX BIG MEN" SWEATING UNDER HEAT FROM CAPED VIGILANTE

By JOHN RHETT THOMAS
– Bugle Staff Reporter

The Angel

The Angel, in action against common street thug.

The Age of the Marvels, the phenomenon capturing the imaginations of the citizenry, with New York City as its epicenter, has no figure more public than the Angel. Currently in the middle of a one-man dragnet to bring to justice the "Six Big Men," the Angel gave an exclusive interview with the Bugle in the hopes of helping the good people of the city understand his motives. "Justice is the cornerstone of civilized life. It is an irreducible element that no free man can live without," said the Angel, his bright, red cape whipping in the stiff wind blowing across this newspaper's rooftop. "The police and other authorities do a great job insuring justice for the people, but I step in when they can do no more, or when the bad actors among them give in to corruption."

The Angel's recent crusade began with the disposal of three of the "Six Big Men," Gus Ronson, Mike Malone and John Dillon, all of whom lay beyond the reach of the law despite alleged activities involving protection rackets and gambling enterprises. The deaths of the three racketeers took place shortly after the mayor impaneled a group of concerned citizens, including Dr. Horace Lang, to advise him on staunching the recent crime wave. Lang recommended the city, which has long been bedeviled by the slippery criminal figures, take advantage of the services of the Angel, a vigilante with the courage and power to take out the seemingly untouchable.

Asked to comment on Lang's appraisal of him, the Angel said, "I am pleased that there are citizens who recognize what I do as having value to the community. Dr. Lang and the mayor have my full support in their efforts, and my promise to help when I can." His next move is to continue to hack away at the ignominious list of "Six Big Men," which has widely been rumored to include alleged fixers such as Trigger Bolo, Dutch Handson and Steve Enkel, as well as the still-unknown "Big Boss" who controls the action of his henchmen in secrecy.

"I have special plans for the Big Boss. He's last on my list... and I promise to be the last thing he ever sees!" The Angel's assuredness stands in stark contrast to the tragic inability of local police to make headway against organized crime and the mob under-

Story continues in *Golden Age Marvel Comics Omnibus Vol. 1 HC.*

NYPD GRADUATES WOMAN CADET

BETTY DEAN NEAR TOP OF HER CLASS, SETTING NEW STANDARDS FOR EXCELLENCE

By DUGAN TRODGLEN *– Bugle Staff Reporter*

Top Police Academy grad Betty Dean, woman.

The New York City Police Department is a close-knit fraternity of men who look out for one another. Well, look out, boys, there's a sassy little lady among your ranks, and she means to make waves! Betty Dean, 27, is a real up-and-comer in the NYPD and doesn't let her gender get in the way. Betty graduated near the top of her class in the police academy of 1937. She received her highest marks in interrogations and other skills related to personal interactions with suspects, witnesses or victims. She also did surprisingly well with some of the physical tests all would-be police officers endure such as marksmanship and running. In the past two years she has made a name for herself with her tough-gal attitude and no-nonsense approach to crime fighting. It's in her blood. "I always looked up to my grandfather, who was a police chief in Rochester," Betty explains, "and when my father moved us to New York City I really saw a need for good law enforcement."

After attending NYU, Betty could not shake the notion that being an officer of the law was her calling, despite the fact that her employment aptitude test suggested she would make the perfect grammar school teacher. "My mother was very supportive," she recalls, "It was her dad who was the policeman, but my father would have none of it. It's not that he didn't think I could do it. He just knew what kind of hurdles a woman would have to jump in order to be viewed as equal." Well, Betty has certainly jumped over those hurdles more than one might think possible from a woman, and by all accounts she has never used her good looks to get to where she is.

When asked where her interest lies were she lucky enough for advancement, Betty says, "I have to admit I like the idea of undercover work. And something that lets me use my swimming skills. I was quite a swimmer in college and would love to put my skills to use. Heck, if I could go undercover as a swimmer, I think that'd be just about perfect!" It sounds like this is

Story continues in *Golden Age Marvel Comics Omnibus Vol. 1 HC.*

CROSS-BORDER "CREATURE" AT CANADIAN BORDER

SLEEPY CAPE VINCENT HOME TO RASH OF SIGHTINGS

By J.C. YORK – Bugle Staff Reporter

Artist's rendition of border invader

CAPE VINCENT, NY – Border officials in Cape Vincent, NY have reported several nighttime encounters over the past month with a short, stocky man, briefly glimpsed sneaking either into or out of the country. Although originally assumed to be a simple smuggler, his multiple appearances and suspicious demeanor have led officials to believe that the man may have a larger agenda.

Reportedly spotted for the first time several weeks ago climbing out of the Lake Ontario waters, the man was confronted by a patrol agent, who asked that his name be withheld, who described him as "husky and wild-haired." "When I first spotted him, he was hunched over and moving like an animal. At first I thought he was a wolf, or other similar creature." The agent also claimed that when he tried to take the border-jumper into custody, he allegedly "growled" at him and fled.

Three nights later, the same agent spotted the border-jumper again; this time headed in the other direction. Although officials cannot confirm that this was the same man, the agent claims he recognized his eyes. "Cold and steely, like glowing sparks ... dangerous, they were. It was the same fellow, sir, I'd stake my life on it."

Although lacking much of the border security of larger cities like Buffalo, Canada's recent entrance into the war with Germany has prompted heightened patrols at all border towns; and unconfirmed reports abound that Cape Vincent officials suspect the man of being a spy or saboteur. The dates in question conform roughly to a series of reported break-ins at three military facilities in upstate New York, however army officials refuse to comment.

Cape Vincent's border patrol has been called out on four separate occasions since then; although they found nothing the first three times, on the fourth they discovered their vehicle with slashed tires and three long cuts into the metal chassis.

Perhaps more disturbing, though, is the possible correlation between the border-jumper and a bar fight in Syracuse that left two dead. According to witnesses, a short man with strange hair brawled with several alleged gangsters in the Moose Jaw Tavern this past weekend. When threatened, he brandished a strange triple-bladed weapon that appeared to have been carved from bone. Witnesses claim that he fought "like a wild animal, clawing at the men" with his wrist-mounted knives. One brawler died on the spot, the other on the way to the hospital shortly thereafter. Syracuse police are still investigating.

Authorities request that anyone with information about these incidents please contact the Cape Vincent Police

Story continues in *Wolverine Omnibus Vol. 1 HC.*

UNIDENTIFIED FLOATING MAN IN TIMES SQUARE

NO EXPLANATION FOR GAUDILY CLAD MAN

By JESS HARROLD – Bugle Staff Reporter

Police are baffled by eyewitness reports of an armored man floating on an invisible chair in Times Square. More than twenty bystanders contacted the authorities claiming to have seen the man, wearing a blue face mask and hovering in front of a neon cola sign in broad daylight early yesterday, but eyewitness reports say the green and purple clad stranger disappeared before police reached the scene.

An official NYPD statement declared, "We received multiple reports of an armored man floating in a reclined position. Two officers attended the scene, but found nothing out of the ordinary. No formal investigation is taking place into the incident."

But, speaking exclusively to the Daily Bugle, Police Captain Philip De Wolff dismissed the incident as a case of imaginations running wild. "Ever since people started reading about flying men and vigilante heroes, we're getting reports of phenomena like these every other day," he said. "People are so excited about these so-called 'Marvels,' they're seeing them everywhere they look. Folks need to keep calm, and let us concentrate on the real crimes."

However, mailman William Lumpkin is adamant he saw the multi-colored mystery man. Lumpkin, 25, was making his morning delivery when, he claims, the unknown figure suddenly appeared on an "invisible" floating chair. Said Lumpkin, "When he appeared out of nowhere, I darn near dropped my mail sack. The guy just sat there, relaxed as anything, in thin air! He must have been twenty feet up, just watching us, like he was sizing us all up. That crazy blue face, smiling as if he could conquer us as soon as look at us.

"He was there five, ten minutes saying nothing. Then, all of a sudden, he said 'not enough of a challenge yet,' then up and disappeared. I could deliver mail until I'm 80, I bet I'll never see anything that fantastic again!"

But not every bystander was impressed by the mysterious stranger. Hotdog vendor Richie Fisk said, "We get it all here, he was nothing special. One guy with a beard did the exact same thing just last week. Man, you shoulda seen the hat on that guy!"

Story continues in *Avengers: Kang Time and Time Again TPB.*

Artist's rendition of Willie Lumpkin's eyewitness account of floating man.

Teen artist Rogers receives C.A.P. Arts medal.

STEVEN ROGERS WINS C.A.P. ARTS AWARD
BROOKLYN TEEN SCOOPS FIRST PRIZE

By JESS HARROLD – *Bugle Staff Reporter*

Coming in first out of more than 1,000 entries, Steve Rogers won the gold medal for the annual Creative Arts Project's prestigious "Artists of the Future" competition, which this year had the topical theme "Dawn of the Marvels." Entrants had to design their own comic book heroes, and produce five pages of them in action. Steven won the day with a sequence showing his patriotic soldier-turned-super-hero, The Sentinel of Liberty, in battle with his arch-foe, the man-without-a-country named The Nomad.

In addition to the medal, Steven, who hopes to study fine arts, wins a week of access to the offices of competition sponsor Timely Publications, where the impressionable boy will have the opportunity to see actual comic book artists at work. In addition, young Steven will receive a year's subscription to Timely's brand new comic title, *Marvel Comics*.

"What a swell deal," replied the shy, young artist when asked to comment on his winnings. "This new *Marvel* publication is full of stories with men in action. It's very inspiring to me!"

Publisher Martin Goodman, the competition's head judge, said it was the dynamism of Steven's work that made him stand out from the crowd. "You wouldn't think of it to look at him, but this scrawny little kid's pages had such power, such action," Mr. Goodman said. "He draws war scenes like he's born for it. And there's a really iconic, symbolic look to his pencils. Inspirational stuff.

"This kid keeps up the good work, and believe me, one day every comic fan will know the name Steve Rogers."

But the modest teen maintained he just got lucky winning first prize. "Gee, I just draw the stuff that's in my head," Steven said. "I don't know if it's anything special. But I'm really pleased Mr. Goodman and the other judges liked my work. Watching real artists like Bill Everett and Carl Burgos at work will be a great honor." Asked about what inspired his creation, the Sentinel of Liberty, Steven added: "I love my country, there's no greater inspiration."

Steven's mother, Sarah Rogers, could barely contain her delight at her son's triumph. "Steven's never been much of a one for sports, he probably couldn't throw a football ten yards," she said. "But he's barely stopped drawing since he learned to hold a pencil. His art has shielded him from some of the rough stuff boys get up to these days. We're all thrilled that his hard work has paid off. I just know my boy's going to create a legacy."

Story continues in *Golden Age Captain America Masterworks Vol. 1 HC.*

PAL FUNDRAISER SCHEDULED FOR SATURDAY
HELL'S KITCHEN ORGANIZATION HELPS TEEN BOYS

By DUGAN TRODGLEN – Bugle Staff Reporter

The New York City Police Athletic League is holding its fall fundraiser/exhibition this Saturday at 10am at their youth facility on 43rd street. As usual, the talents of many young area men will be on display to showcase the excellent work the PAL does with neighborhood boys in the field of fitness. Director Jason Morgan is quick to remind us that physical excellence is not the whole story, however. "We pride ourselves on helping these young men get a good education to go along with their athletic achievement," Morgan says with a fatherly pride in his eyes. "I don't think we'd be worth two hoots if we weren't doing our best to help these boys achieve as much as they can in life. Some of these boys came to us nearly failing out of school and with our mentoring and tutoring are now making A's and B's."

It will be athletics that will be on display Saturday, however. The young men are eager to show off their skills. One especially confident high school senior actually approached us during my interview with Morgan. "Pardon me, Ma'am, but I'm Nicholas Fury," the handsome youth said, "and I think your readers should know I'm going to be boxing Timothy Daniels on Saturday and I'm going to knock him out!" Playing along, I responded, "Is that right?" to which he replied "That's right, Ma'am, and I'm also a sure thing to win the archery tournament!" I asked Nicholas how PAL had helped him. "They've helped me be sure of myself and taught me that I can do anything... anything I decide I want to do." When asked what he thinks he wants to do, the young man naturally had an answer ready: "I'm going to be a man of action. I may join the army. I believe in doing my duty and I love this country. After that, all I know is I'm going to do things most people only read about."

Morgan laughs as he runs Nicholas off, but tells me he loves the boy's enthusiasm, saying, "He's cocky, but he's right. That Nick Fury is one to keep an eye out for." He tells me the

Story continues in *Marvel Masterworks: Sgt. Fury Vol. 1 HC.*

Nicholas Fury (right) proudly displaying target, presented marksman's ribbon by Sgt. Fred O'Neill (left)

"FLYING SAUCER" SIGHTINGS WORRY NEW JERSEY TOWN

CONNECTION SOUGHT TO PREVIOUS INCIDENT?

By J.C. YORK – Bugle Staff Reporter

Missing mobster "Machine Gun" Martin.

MORRISTOWN, NJ – Local residents have recently reported a rash of sightings of a large metallic craft flying through the New Jersey skies. Several residents have described it as cylindrical, with a round flat underside, a large raised bump on the top and multiple lights ringing the sides, moving at great speed, or hovering in place over various wooded areas.

Longtime resident Douglas Errol, who has reported sighting the object near his home on four consecutive nights, described it as resembling a "flying saucer ... about fifteen or twenty feet across, rotating and making odd humming sounds." Speculation immediately ran to some sort of small Zeppelin, but no landing strips in the area still service the cumbersome vehicles, and Errol maintains that the ship's speed far outstrips that of a Zeppelin. Local police and military officials report that they are "looking into the sightings," but deny any involvement and declined to make any further statements.

Interestingly, descriptions of the craft match those recorded by prison officials and policemen four years ago in upstate New York, during a prison breakout by convicted killer and reputed mobster John "Machine Gun" Martin. Martin was the subject of a countywide manhunt after his escape, but just as authorities believed they had him cornered in a remote marsh, many officers of the law on site reported seeing a dimly lit, disc-shaped vehicle rise from the ground and take off "at fantastic speed ... straight up until we lost sight of it." Martin was never found, and the vehicle was assumed to be some sort of getaway craft arranged by his fellow gangsters – although over the years, as dime-novel "science-fiction" stories of moon men and spacecrafts have risen in popularity, more fanciful explanations for the craft's origins have been offered.

Errol ascribes to the latter interpretation. "It's men from other worlds. I've no doubt about it. They took Martin then, and they've come back for more of us! They've come back for me!" Errol has made several attempts to speak to Morristown's city council, but lost much credibility when he claimed that the craft landed in his neighbor's backyard, and a "little green man" emerged and transformed into the shape of his neighbor, the widow Ruby Tucker. Errol was cited for public drunkenness and city officials are urging calm.

The "saucer" has not been seen for the last two nights. However, when this reporter returned to Errol's home to ask his opinion about its absence, he was unable to be located. It is assumed that Errol has left town to visit relatives and calm his nerves, and this paper will seek a follow-up

Story continues in *Fantastic Four Masterworks Vol. 9 HC* and *Secret Invasion: The Infiltration TPB.*

Artist's conception of Morristown's "flying saucers."

WILD WEST EXHIBIT COMES TO MANHATTAN

EXPLORES HISTORY OF RAWHIDE KID, OTHER CLASSIC GUNFIGHTERS

By JOHN RHETT THOMAS – Bugle Staff Reporter

Johnny Bart, the Rawhide Kid, is one of America's Marvels of the Old West.

The Wild West comes alive at a special installation at the Met this weekend, curated by the Sons of Stagecoach Gap, a historical society from Dodge City, Kansas. The exhibit, *America's Marvels of the Old West*, showcases the cowboys and gunslingers of the pioneer days, with a special focus on four of the most famous, Kid Colt, the Two-Gun Kid, the Rawhide Kid, and the Masked Raider.

"Our goal is to reveal the hardscrabble life of the gunmen of the range," said exhibit spokesman Jack Keller. "In our modern, more urban world, with its many comforts and technological achievements, it's often hard to relate to those seemingly outmoded ways of life. The true exploits of the lone man on horseback, wandering the prairies and deserts in pursuit of justice, often seem more like worlds of fantasy when we read about them in history books or in entertainment fare such as *Marvel Mystery Comics*."

To that end, the exhibit brings to the fore the armaments, the outfits, the horse tack and the historic legacy of the cowboys. "These men risked death on a daily basis," commented Keller. "So to get a look at the implements used to keep them alive in a dangerous world gives us fascinating insights into the human condition."

Also included in the exhibit are vintage newspaper articles mounted for easy reading. For instance, the Rawhide Kid's showdown in Trigger Gap with the Garson Gang, one of his earliest exploits, is recorded in detail, revealing the Kid's courage under fire as he defended the small town from thuggish bandits. In addition, the personal diaries of Susan Clark, the young daughter of Trigger Gap's sheriff, describe her personal interactions with the dashing young gunman, as well as his awkward attempts at forging a relationship with her. "Young Johnny Bart always attracted the attention of the ladies. For some reason, he just didn't hold on to any of them," remarked Keller.

Perhaps the most impressive feature of the exhibit is the authentic totem rumored to have gone on a rampage of destruction near Abilene, Texas. Recovered from the bottom of Bottomless Canyon, the "Terrible Totem" stands at nearly 20 feet tall, its finely crafted wooden shell riddled with bullets from the Rawhide Kid's pistols.

America's Marvels of the Old West will be at the Met through December, and it is made possible with a sponsorship from Howard Stark, whose interest in the can-do spirit of the American individual has led to his own breakthroughs as an inventor and his beneficence as a

Story continues in *Rawhide Kid Masterworks Vols. 1-2 HC.*

VAN DYNE UNVEILS LATEST LINE

NEW LOOKS REPEL RAIN, ATTRACT ATTENTION

By SHEILA JOHNSON – Bugle Fashion Editor

On Tuesday morning, visitors and spectators near the Hotel Winchester were treated to perhaps the most unusual fashion show ever seen outside of Paris. Five models wearing tailored capes, elegant shawls, and sleek hats pranced along the sidewalk in front of the hotel as if the cement were a catwalk. Their smiles were bright, their outfits unwrinkled.

Close by, pedestrians and members of the press applauded while being soaked by a terrible thunderstorm.

Textile magnate Blaine van Dyne grinned as raindrops literally bounced off of his models' coats, leaving the fabric perfectly dry. "That fabric is designed to repel rain, hail, bullets of a certain caliber, and electromagnetic radiation," he declared. "The pieces themselves – well, they're just designed to stun!"

Although the look of the line was conceived by designer Amelia van Dyne, who is also Mr. van Dyne's wife and business partner, the material used to make the pieces was created with the help of an unlikely collaborator: Mr. van Dyne's brother,

Fashion parade at Hotel Winchester.

research scientist Vernon van Dyne. "I just see this as finally putting Vernon's work to good use," the textile giant quipped.

After the spontaneous sidewalk show, the five young women continued into the hotel, where they would model the outerwear for Mr. van Dyne's prospective clients: the wives of senators, representatives, and foreign diplomats. He hoped that orders would be placed even though researchers were still trying to fix one design flaw: "We are still concerned about the fabric's long-term resistance to moths and other insects," he confessed.

Designer Amelia Van Dyne at work.

Story continues in *Ant-Man / Giant-Man Masterworks Vol. 1 HC.*

HANOVER AGENCY PUTS OUT TALENT CALL

ESTEEMED AGENCY SEEKS TO EXPAND

By JOHN RHETT THOMAS – Bugle Fashion Editor

Fashion houses the world over have begun relying on the upstart Hanover Agency to fill their personnel needs by filling their fashion attire with some of modeling's most intriguing new talent. After all, the dresses, coats, accessories and millinery that fill the best department stores don't show themselves, and as Hanover executives are quick to point out, it takes a special kind of model to reveal the finer points of women's fashion to a world hungry for hot new trends.

Another thing this burgeoning new company is quick to point out is that their talent is expressly geared to meet the challenges of the coming decade of haute couture. There is always a need for the new, however, and to that end, the Hanover Agency is holding an open call for models at their Garment District headquarters to fill a wide range of modeling personnel needs.

"We're looking for blondes, brunettes, redheads," said talent scout Ruth Atkinson as we caught up with her eyeing the parade of talent at this year's Little Miss Brisket Pageant. "A Hanover girl is a versatile girl, one who can display the essence of any outfit with minimal effort. She has to be able to tell a story, helping bring a woman's imagination to life with adventure, romance, and even a bit of humor, every time they see her modeling a client's fashion."

Asked if she had seen any potential Hanover talent on display at the pageant, Atkinson replied, "Patsy Walker, Hedy Wolfe... They have bright futures ahead of them. I'm not sure if they're Hanover material, but I can easily see them as Miss Americas!" Instead, Atkinson's eyes were most focused on a young runner-up named Millicent Collins, a blonde beauty who lost out despite formidable baton-twirling skills and the polished poise of a runway model. "Now *that's* a Hanover girl. I need to make sure she's aware of our open call!"

Story continues in *Models, Inc. #1.*

WALKER BEATS OUT WOLFE FOR PAGEANT CROWN

AUDIENCE, JUDGES, "HEAD OVER HEELS" FOR DARLING REDHEAD

By SHEILA JOHNSON – Bugle Fashion Editor

Miss Patsy Walker, this year's Little Miss Brisket.

Last week, Huntsford Fine Butcher and Delicatessen held its annual competition in search of the next darling face to sell its choice cuts.

The Little Miss Brisket Pageant drew forty-two entrants from five schools. The prospective princesses of prime rib competed in four categories: Formal Wear, Casual Wear, Question and Answer, and Talent.

Although Hedy Wolfe, 14, performed a bright and airy rendition of "America the Beautiful" that left many in the audience murmuring their approval, she was followed in the "Talent" portion by Patsy Walker, 14. The red-haired Miss Walker performed a gymnastics routine so energized that audience members in the front row leaned back lest her cartwheels land her in one of their laps. The roar of wild applause for Miss Walker presupposed the results. R. Bentley Huntsford, owner of the store, dubbed her "a little firecracker" as he crowned her Little Miss Brisket 1939. Miss Wolfe was first runner-up.

Miss Walker's prize winnings were five dollars and a pound of brisket delivered to

her family's home once a month for the next year.

The "little firecracker" can already be seen in her role as Little Miss Brisket at Huntsford's butcher shop, where a poster featuring an artist's rendition of Miss Walker in her costume for the "Talent" portion hangs in the storefront window. Customers reported that the poster initially caused confusion because Mr. Huntsford, upon receiving the print, promptly hung it in the window upside-down. Patrons of his delicatessen assumed that the meat had been oriented as a conscious decision, perhaps intended to conjure images of Miss Walker's electrifying backflips. Only when a customer spoke to Mr. Huntsford, commending him on his eye-catching advertising, did the meat magnate realize his mistake and hang the poster correctly.

According to a witness, Mr. Huntsford response was, "What can I say? We're just head over heels about Patsy!"

Story continues in *Patsy Walker, Hellcat TPB.*

IRONY OF HORTON'S DEATH EASY TO PREDICT

By The Editors Of The Daily Bugle

In March of this year, the Daily Bugle was witness to another example of the threat inherent in rampant scientific advances that don't adhere to society's moral values. This paper led the call for the destruction of the so-called Human Torch. We immediately recognized the threat of not just a creature that lives engulfed in flames, but of the very idea of creating artificial life. That the first example of man's attempt to play God resulted in this tragedy should come as a surprise to no one.

In a March 13 editorial, the Daily Bugle printed an open letter to the now deceased Professor Phineas Horton, warning him of the dangerous path he was on, and we were hardly the lone voice of reason. Virtually the entire scientific community condemned Horton's creation, as well as his decision to create his flaming abomination without the input of his peers, waiting until far too late to request help and advice from fellow scientists. It was an example of the arrogance at the heart of so much science, and ultimately the cause of Horton's own demise. Worst of all, Horton's death may not be the last his creation causes. Indeed, while the deaths of crime boss Anthony Sardo and several associates may not cause many tears to be shed among the law enforcement community, if the body count is attributable to the Human Torch, it is a dangerous sign of things to come, as alleged "heroes" bearing might that our police and military forces must marvel at cause havoc and mayhem as unelected, uncommissioned, and undesired vigilantes.

Scientists should be content to merely be scientists and leave the evolution of mankind to God or fate.

Prof. Horton unveils Human Torch.

LETTERS TO THE EDITOR

I know there's been a lot of controversy about these costumed crusaders who have shown up these last few weeks, but I for one welcome them to our city. The hoods and the criminals are getting more dangerous by the day, and our police can only do so much. With heroes like the Angel and the Human Torch stepping forward to protect us, this Age of Marvels is destined to be a new era of prosperity. I can only dream of what the world will be like for my children, and my children's children, if colorful characters like these are embraced by our society.
Richard Jones

I live on an army base, and wonder why we're waiting so gosh darn long to get over there and fix Hitler's wagon! By golly, we need to take action, and go after Adolf before he comes after us.
James Barnes (aged 13)

When are the cops going to do something to clean up Yancy Street? The hoodlums are out of control, it's getting so bad I don't want to let my niece Petunia out of the house. I've seen the way they look at her...
Penelope Williams

Something needs to be done urgently about these costumed vigilantes that are infesting our streets. I do not want to raise my children in a world where these abhorrent individuals lord over us, as if we are a lesser species. God created this world for mankind, not these super-powered abominations. What if their demonic abilities are somehow infectious? What if our own children are tainted by them? If we act now, and demand that they register themselves and submit to regulation and control, we may be able to prevent our whole society from being overrun by walking crimes against nature. I applaud the Bugle's continued skepticism about these so-called "heroes" in our midst. But I urge you to go further, and stand up for all humanity by seeking to stamp out these "Marvels" now, before it's too late.
Andrew Stryker

I read with great interest the news in your international edition about the so-called Marvels, whose fantastic powers have so captured your attention. Of course, the development of individuals with such unique skills was an inevitability, as my own unique studies in the field of genetics and biology have shown for many years. There is nothing unnatural at work, simply evolution taking its next great lurch into the unknown. I await with extreme interest the abilities that humanity will manifest over the coming years.
Nathaniel Essex (London, England)

BIRTHS

Record of recent births in New York City and surrounding areas.

PARKER
To Peter and Ann Parker, a baby boy, Ben, weighing in at a healthy 8 pounds 3 ounces. Welcome to the world our very own great responsibility!

RICHARDS
Major John Richards and his wife Laura proudly announce the birth of their son Nathaniel, weighing 7 pounds 11 ounces. Fingers crossed for a fantastic future.

REILLY
To Hector and Anna Reilly of Brooklyn, New York, a daughter, May, born on 5 May, weighing 6 pounds 2 ounces. A fragile little thing, but with plenty of heart!

ROSS
General Alexander Ross and his wife Elizabeth are proud to announce the birth of their son Thaddeus, at a whopping 8 pounds 5 ounces. Daddy's little thunderbolt!

GRIMM
A son for Benjamin and Mary, a younger brother for Jacob, bashful, blue-eyed Daniel weighs in at 7 pounds, 13 ounces. Our little "idol of millions."

FORBUSH
Stan and Jacqueline Forbush announce the birth of a son, Irving, weighing 7 pounds 2 ounces, on Friday 13th. They wanted a daughter.

DAILY BUGLE

EDITOR: John Rhett Thomas
PHOTOGRAPHERS: Phil Sheldon, Chance Fiveash
COVER PHOTO: Mike Mayhew
LAYOUT: Brian O'Dell
STAFF REPORTERS: Jess Harrold, Sheila Johnson, Dugan Trodglen, Jeph York
RESEARCH: Bob Greenberger